Oksana Kim

THE EFFECTS AND IMPLICATIONS OF KAZAKHSTAN'S ADOPTION OF INTERNATIONAL FINANCIAL REPORTING STANDARDS

A Resource Dependence Perspective

With a foreword by Svetlana Vlady

ibidem-Verlag
Stuttgart

Bibliografische Information der Deutschen Nationalbibliothek
Die Deutsche Nationalbibliothek verzeichnet diese Publikation in der Deutschen Nationalbibliografie; detaillierte bibliografische Daten sind im Internet über http://dnb.d-nb.de abrufbar.

Bibliographic information published by the Deutsche Nationalbibliothek
Die Deutsche Nationalbibliothek lists this publication in the Deutsche Nationalbibliografie; detailed bibliographic data are available in the Internet at http://dnb.d-nb.de.

Cover picture: © Doris Rieck. Source: Wikimedia Commons. Licensed under CC BY 3.0.
(s. https://creativecommons.org/licenses/by-sa/3.0/de/deed.en)

∞

Gedruckt auf alterungsbeständigem, säurefreien Papier
Printed on acid-free paper

ISSN: 1614-3515

ISBN-13: 978-3-8382-0987-6

© *ibidem*-Verlag
Stuttgart 2017

Alle Rechte vorbehalten

Das Werk einschließlich aller seiner Teile ist urheberrechtlich geschützt. Jede Verwertung außerhalb der engen Grenzen des Urheberrechtsgesetzes ist ohne Zustimmung des Verlages unzulässig und strafbar. Dies gilt insbesondere für Vervielfältigungen, Übersetzungen, Mikroverfilmungen und elektronische Speicherformen sowie die Einspeicherung und Verarbeitung in elektronischen Systemen.

All rights reserved. No part of this publication may be reproduced, stored in or introduced into a retrieval system, or transmitted, in any form, or by any means (electronic, mechanical, photocopying, recording or otherwise) without the prior written permission of the publisher. Any person who does any unauthorized act in relation to this publication may be liable to criminal prosecution and civil claims for damages.

Printed in the EU

To my family

Table of Contents

List of Tables ... 9
List of Figures ... 11
Foreword by Svetlana Vlady ... 13
Chapter 1. Introduction ... 15
Chapter 2. Background information. ... 23
    2.1. Kazakhstan's history and development after the collapse of the Soviet Union ... 23
    2.2. Capital market reforms and adoption of International Financial Reporting Standards (IFRS) in Kazakhstan. ... 38
        2.2.1. National stock market system ... 38
    2.2. Adoption of International Financial Reporting Standards (IFRS) in Kazakhstan ... 45

Chapter 3. Global adoption of IFRS ... 49
    3.1. History behind the global movement to adopt a uniform set of accounting standards and the evolvement of IFRS ... 49
    3.2. Empirical evidence regarding implementation of IFRS: economic and legal explanations to the degree of success of IFRS adoption ... 54
    3.3. Alternative explanations to the IFRS adoption consequences, not limited by legal and economic arguments. Evidence regarding the IFRS adoption benefits for CIS countries ... 57

Chapter 4. Resource dependence theory and its application to Kazakhstan's strategic decision to become the first and early adopter of IFRS within the CIS ... 61
    4.1. The main provisions of the Resource Dependence Theory ... 61
    4.2. Application of the Resource Dependence Theory to Kazakhstan's strategic decision to become the first adopter of IFRS within the CIS ... 65

Chapter 5. Empirical Analyses 79
    5.1. Value relevance of reported information
          in the post-adoption period 80
    5.2. Comparison of value relevance of reported information
          for Kazakhstani and Russian public firms 91
    5.3. Examining changes in market efficiency over time, before
          and after IFRS adoption, using the KASE index 94
          5.2.1. Autocorrelation Test 96
          5.2.2. The unit root test 97
    5.4. Kazakhstani blue chips cross-listed in London:
          The market reaction to the cross-listing event 100

Chapter 6. Future perspectives. 113
    6.1. Kazakhstan's success and future perspectives 113
    6.2. The future of the IFRS reporting practices
          in Kazakhstan 115

Chapter 7. Conclusions 119

Bibliography 121

List of Tables

Table 1. GDP and GDP per capita for Kazakhstan and Russia over 1995–2011. 31

Table 2. Total volume of exports and the export annual growth rate for Kazakhstan and Russia. 36

Table 3. Global Competitiveness Indicators for Kazakhstan and Russia (2015). 37

Table 4. Listing destinations and origins of public companies affiliated with Kazakhstan (Datastream). 43

Table 5. Market capitalization of domestic listed firms for Kazakhstan (Datastream). 43

Table 6. Foreign Aid and Foreign Direct Investment for Kazakhstan and Russia. 71

Table 7. List of Kazakhstani public companies used in the empirical analyses: 41 public firms and 237 firm-year observations for which data on Price, EPS and BVPS were available in Datastream. 83

Table 8. Descriptive Statistics. 88

Table 9. Empirical Analyses—value relevance of reported information post adoption of IFRS. 89

Table 10. Empirical Analyses—changes in value relevance of information post 2011 91

Table 11. Comparative reporting quality for Kazakhstani versus Russian public firms. 94

Table 12. Serial correlation test for KASE daily returns. Examined period: December 2000-April 2016. 99

Table 13. Properties of KASE returns series. Examined period: December 2000–April 2016. 100

Table 14. Comparative reporting obligations for exchange-listed ADRs and GDRs. 103

List of Figures

Figure 1. Upper picture: GDP per capita growth, Kazakhstan versus CIS. 1992–2014. Lower picture: Global competitiveness of Kazakhstan compared to other CIS states....34

Figure 2. Historical monthly correlation between KASE and MICEX share price indices: August 2000–April 2016...................77

Figure 3. Kazmunajgas' post-listing CARs. 109

Figure 4. Halyk Bank's post-listing CARs. 109

Figure 5. Kazakhstan Kagazy's post-listing CARs. 110

Figure 6. Alliance Bank's post-listing CARs..............................110

Foreword

The adoption of International Financial Reporting Standards (IFRS) is expected to enhance the quality of financial reports and improve the scope of cross-border business transactions. To date, more than 140 nations have committed to adopt IFRS. Nevertheless, the outcome of this reform remains uncertain, especially for emerging markets, such as the countries of the former Soviet Union. The extant literature provides limited evidence on pros and cons of the IFRS adoption process for the transitional economies, such as Kazakhstan.

After the collapse of the Soviet Union, in 1990s, the radical economic reforms implemented in the former Soviet countries would not have been possible without the assistance of major external donors, such as the International Monetary Fund (IMF) and the World Bank. The adoption of IFRS was one of the requirements of the assistance package offered by the IMF and the World Bank. In early 1990s, the former Soviet nations were in competition to attract foreign direct investment. Kazakhstan was the first former Soviet nation to implement radical capital market reforms, such as adoption of IFRS. Moreover, Kazakhstan adopted IFRS in 2004–2005, ahead of the European Union, Russia, and other leading emerging markets. However, Kazakhstan's reforms, including the adoption of IFRS, have received limited attention in the literature, and it is the Russian market that has historically attracted experts' attention, among the former Soviet Union countries.

This book adopts the resource dependence theory and empirically examines the outcomes of the reforms that the government of Kazakhstan undertook towards the formation of the capital market system. The capital market reforms in Kazakhstan mirrored the Russian reforms, due to the similar environmental dependencies that the two nations faced after the collapse of the Soviet Union. Critics argued that the reforms in Kazakhstan, including the adoption of IFRS, were premature and would negatively impact the capital market system and the economy of Kazakhstan, as the country has limited resources and an underdeveloped infrastructure. However, the author reports that adoption of IFRS resulted in a significant inflow of foreign capital to Kazakhstan and benefited Kazakhstani public firms. Therefore, this book's findings are inconsistent with studies that have shown that the adoption of IFRS would inevitably be unsuccessful if implemented without adequate supporting infrastructure and within a short timeframe.

The book also discusses the prospects for Kazakhstan's stock market, economic model, and strategic development plan, all of which emphasize the importance of foreign investment to the national economy, and the prospects for the integration of the Kazakhstani economy into the global market system. The new economic model is based on the promotion of the private sector, free competition, and the development of the national stock market. The conclusion the author offers is that Kazakhstan has become an effective state with an independent history and is placed among the most progressive emerging markets. Overall, this book provides valuable insight for standard setters, academic researchers, and government institutions that promote the harmonization of accounting standards and practices across the globe.

Dr Svetlana Vlady
Brooklyn College, The City University of New York

Chapter 1. Introduction

> "WE ARE IN FOR A NEW CENTURY,
> NEW TIMES ARE COMING..."
>
> *Virgil*

The aim of this book is to examine the decision, timing, strategy and consequences of the International Financial Reporting Standards (IFRS) adoption reform in a previously unexplored emerging market, the constituent of the former Soviet Union—Kazakhstan. I rely on the *resource dependence* theory of Pfeffer and Salancik (1978) and step away from the economic and legal explanations dominating the extant IFRS-based literature (Ball et al. 2000, 2003; La Porta et al. 1997, 2000), therefore analyzing the IFRS adoption and other capital market reforms in Kazakhstan through a different lens. In its originality, the resource dependence theory is deeply rooted in sociology and attempts to explain the behavior of organizations operating under the influence of a wide array of external factors (pressures), the most significant being resource interdependence with various stakeholders.

The resource dependence theory rests on a number of assumptions: first, firms are constrained by the resource interdependence with other organizations whose actions are uncertain, which leads to a situation in which a firm's continual survival and success are also uncertain. Second, firms have to take actions to manage those external dependencies, which may or may not be successful and, in turn, can produce other forms of interdependence (Pfeffer 1987). To some extent, uncertainty can be dismantled by a firm's engaging in cooperative (coalition) activities with its stakeholders (Ulrich and Barney 1984). When cooperating actions are no longer efficient, a firm may take unilateral actions and, through political mechanisms, create an environment that is better for its own interest (Pfeffer and Salancik 1978), but is not necessarily best for its stakeholders with whom it shares resources.

Despite the popularity of this framework in organizational and strategic management research, it has received limited application in other disciplines such as accounting, finance and economics (Hillman et al. 2009). This theory, nevertheless, provides a new, unexplored, context for analyzing a nation's decision, timing and strategy to adopt IFRS and implement concurrent capital market reforms. After the collapse of the Soviet Union in 1991 and formation of the Commonwealth of the Independent States (CIS), several nations that had previously been managed through a central command system faced a dilemma regarding how to build an independent capital market system while still experiencing a high level of resource interdependence among each other. Indeed, during the Soviet Union era the customer and supplier chain for the extracting industry that made the highest contribution towards the country's GDP was spread across several republics. After 1991, however, each newly independent nation was left with a piece of the previously unified production system. More importantly, while there was a clear need to form economic cooperation mechanisms among the nations in order to survive, each nation started facing a competition from others as a result of the necessity to attract external capital. Within the CIS, the Russian Federation and Kazakhstan were the leading nations that pioneered capital market reforms, including adoption of IFRS. Other CIS nations, however, were significantly behind in terms of the economic, social and political development.

Kazakhstan was the first CIS nation to implement the IFRS adoption reform, to the surprise of critics and the global investment community. The steps of Kazakhstan's government towards formation of the capital market system paralleled those of the country's closest economic partner—Russia. In essence, the capital market reforms in Kazakhstan mimicked those of Russia and were implemented shortly after reforms were put into place in Russia. The resource dependence theory posits that players (in this case, nations) that operate in comparable regulatory environments, have related backgrounds, and face similar constraints, are likely to implement the same political actions (in this case, capital market reforms) (Pfeffer and Salancik 1978). This proposition was empirically tested in Mullery et al. (1995) who found that firms in comparable regulatory environments had similar patterns in political contributions. Therefore, the fact that the capital market reforms in Kazakhstan mirrored those of Russia is not surprising and is due to the similar environmental dependencies that the two nations faced after the collapse of the Soviet Union (in 1990s). Moreover, the parallelism in capital market reforms can be viewed as a *cooperating* mechanism between the two nations. Blumenritt and Nigh (2002), for example, documented that similar resource dependence is a predictor of coordination of political actions among subsidiaries of a multinational firm.

The above noted cooperation in market reforms that started in the early 1990s between Russia and Kazakhstan only existed in the first decade of their independence, until approximately 2003. Clearly, the CIS countries were not the only major stakeholders affecting each other's economic development. The CIS nations were in stiff competition with each other to attract Foreign Direct Investments (FDIs) and get assistance from foreign donors. The radical economic reforms implemented in the CIS nations would not be possible without the assistance of the major external donors, such as the International Monetary Fund (IMF) and the World Bank. By 2003, there was a significant disparity in economic development of Kazakhstan compared to Russia, and the former's need for FDIs and hence external resource dependence was more substantial compared to Russia. The two countries experienced diverse financial needs. Russia became significantly more successful, compared to Kazakhstan, in restoring the national economy and securing internal resources for development of the capital markets system. Therefore, by 2003, Kazakhstan's reliance on external stakeholders—foreign donors—became more significant than interdependence with the Russian economy. The resource dependence theory, while recognizing the importance of both the internal and external contingencies (stakeholders), is silent about which form of dependence takes precedence over others in situations where multiple dependencies exist (Hillman et al. 2009). Nevertheless, the related *stakeholder theory* provides a constructive frame for identifying "primary" versus "secondary" stakeholders. Mitchell et al. (1997) suggest that this classification and stakeholder precedence should be formed based on the three attributes of power, legitimacy and urgency. As will be discussed in details in the next chapters, by early 2000s, all three attributes were greater in the case of external donors and hence, Kazakhstan's pressure from the external stakeholders was more significant than that from Russia.

The adoption of IFRS is one of the necessary conditions supporting the inflow of external resources (Chen et al. 2014) and is typically a part of the requirements of the external assistance package from the IMF and the World Bank (Ashraf and Ghani 2005, Solodchenko and Sucher 2005). In 2004 Russia first announced, and subsequently reverted from, the IFRS adoption plan, until revisiting it in 2010. Kazakhstan, nevertheless, decided to proceed with this reform and became the first CIS nation to implement the IFRS adoption initiative within a short timeframe. This was done in response to the external pressure from foreign capital providers that took precedence over internal interdependencies with Russia. Indeed, as noted by Pfeffer and Salancik (1978), in order to manage external resource dependence, "the organization, through political actions (in this case, IFRS adoption reform), attempts to create for itself an environment that is better for its interest". Overall, beginning in 2003, the competition between Kazakhstan and Russia for external resources gradually replaced the cooperating mechanisms that existed in the 1990s.

Lastly, building on the resource dependency theory and findings in Alon and Dwyer (2014), it appears that the most appropriate strategy for Kazakhstan was to *require*, as opposed to *permit* or *do not allow*, IFRS. This is explained not only by Kazakhstan's heavy reliance on FDIs but also by the fact that Kazakhstan was ranked very low in the early 2000s on the level of informational transparency and corporate governance system, compared to Russia and other emerging markets.

This book contributes to several streams of research. First, I depart from purely economic and legal explanations of the IFRS adoption success that dominate extant literature, such as legal system, tax and ownership laws, and shareholder rights (Ball et al. 2003, Ball 2006, La Porta et al. 1997, 2000)[1]. The findings of the prior literature are inconclusive and provide evidence both in favor of and against the IFRS adoption success, which motivates my empirical investigation. Examining the economic consequences of the IFRS adoption reform for emerging markets, such as Kazakhstan, that possess strikingly different backgrounds and that are fundamentally different from developed countries that went through relatively similar stages of economic development, requires juxtaposing existing theories with other theoretical lenses that could provide more promising explanations for the IFRS adoption consequences. The unique experimental settings of the former Soviet Union nations provide valuable opportunities for this. This study shed light on the multiplicity of the interdependence mechanisms, as well as the precedence that some forms of contingencies take over others when it comes to implementation of capital market reforms in a previously closed market, therefore making a contribution to both the resource dependence theory and also the IFRS adoption literature.

Second, Kazakhstan's capital market reforms, including adoption of IFRS, have received limited attention in prior literature. The most relevant study is by Tyrrall et al. (2007) and it examines the relevance of IFRS implementation to Kazakhstan's economy on a broad level. The authors conclude that the country had no choice but to proceed with IFRS adoption and that over time major obstacles to this process will be overcome, although the changes take pace very slowly due to the communist past of the country. No other studies, to my knowledge, analyzed capital market reforms in Kazakhstan and this is the first work to support the arguments regarding the IFRS adoption benefits to this country by empirical findings.

---

1   Literature also relied on the "cultural" explanation for the IFRS value relevance. Based on Nobes (1998), adoption of IFRS is more likely to be successful in "culturally self-sufficient" (primarily developed) countries, compared to "culturally dominated" (developing) countries. While this is certainly a useful perspective adopted in earlier studies, it does not explain the variation in the IFRS adoption strategies, timing of, and consequences within emerging markets, which is the focus of a more recent stream of literature in international accounting.

Particularly, I demonstrate that reported information is value relevant to investors in the post adoption period, lending support to the IFRS adoption reform. Furthermore, Kazakhstani public firms subject to the IFRS adoption requirement reported information that was more value relevant to investors, compared to their Russian counterparts that did not adopt IFRS. Additionally, the value relevance of information reported by Kazakhstani public firms increased over time. While the Russian market historically attracted attention of researchers, it was Kazakhstan that implemented the progressive capital market reforms first—the finding that remains unexplored in accounting literature and which I further explore in this book, complementing the emerging markets stream of literature.

Third, this work contributes to the discussion regarding the optimal timing for the IFRS adoption reform. The leading role in the IFRS adoption process belonged to developed nations with common law traditions that had a significant supporting infrastructure and legal foundations to adopt IFRS successfully (Barth et al. 2008, 2012). The case of Kazakhstan, nevertheless, was unique in that the national government chose to adopt IFRS in 2004–2005, even ahead of the European Union and before Russia and other leading emerging markets. Critics argued that such a decision was premature and would negatively impact the economy and the capital market system of Kazakhstan, as the country had limited resources. Tyrrall et al. (2007) suggested that because of the communist past with a strong command system, IFRS adoption was hurting public companies and the long-term consequences of this reform were unpredictable. The authors concluded that environmental differences between Kazakhstan and other European countries "provide little or no justification for the relevance of IFRS" (p. 99). I report that the IFRS adoption reform, on a contrary, resulted in significant inflow of foreign capital and also benefited Kazakhstani public firms. This study's findings, therefore, are inconsistent with the studies showing that IFRS adoption would inevitably be unsuccessful if implemented without proper supporting infrastructure and within a short timeframe (e.g., Karampinis and Hevas 2011).

The book proceeds as follows. Chapter 2 provides the background information on Kazakhstan and discusses the economic processes beginning in 1991 until the present day, with emphasis on capital market reforms. In chapter 3 I provide a brief overview of the history of the global adoption of IFRS and also summarize empirical findings that shed light on economic consequences of this reform among various nations and categories of companies. I begin chapter 4 with discussing the resource dependence theory of Pfeffer and Salancik (1978) in its originality and I provide an overview of the empirical findings of the studies that relied on this framework to explain behavior and choices of organizations. I then analyze the strategy, timing and choice of the Kazakhstani government related to IFRS adoption. In chapter 5, I perform a battery of empirical tests: first, I show that following adoption of IFRS, earnings and book value of Kazakhstani public firms are value relevant to investors; second, I report that during the period of 2005–2011, the quality of reporting information was higher in the case of Kazakhstani public firms that were required to use IFRS, compared to their Russian peers that did not use IFRS; third, I document that despite the course of capital market reforms, there was no improvement in informational efficiency of Kazakhstan's stock market; finally, I show that investors reacted positively (except for one case) to listing in London by Kazakhstani firms that reported in accordance with IFRS. In chapter 6, I discuss future perspectives of Kazakhstan, and chapter 7 concludes the book.

Chapter 2. Background information

2.1. Kazakhstan's history and development after the collapse of the Soviet Union

Modern Kazakhstan is a unique nation in many respects. The country is the ninth largest nation in geographic area and occupies both the European and Asian territories; it is the world's largest landlocked nation. Therefore, Kazakhstan provides important trade routes from Asia to Europe and is considered "the Silk route" to the European continent (Erns and Young 2015). The territory of Kazakhstan exceeds that of Western Europe, although the population density is among the lowest in the world. Kazakhstan possesses enormous resources of fossil fuels and other minerals and metals, including uranium, copper and zinc (LOC, CIA 2013). Consequently, extractive industries have been the central component of Kazakhstan's economy. Kazakhstan has been heavily involved in exporting natural resources and grain to its major neighbors, primarily the former republics of the Soviet Union, of which Russia remains Kazakhstan's major trade partner.

Interestingly, Kazakhstan is the only former Soviet Union republic where the indigenous ethnic group did not constitute the majority of the population upon dissolution of the Soviet Union. By 1994, only 44 percent of the population were native Kazakhs, whereas Russians and other Slavic nations accounted for about 45 percent (LOC, CIA 2013)[2]. Remarkably, Kazakhstan is known for the significant number of minority population groups, including Germans, Koreans, Jewish, Tatars and Uyghurs, primarily a result of the historical processes, particularly Stalin's repressions in the

---

2   The demographic situation changed over time due to migration of the Russian population to nearby CIS states, primarily Russia, and as a result, the local (Kazakh) population now accounts for about 64 percent. Russian population constitutes approximately 23 percent.

1930s[3]. The state language of Kazakhstan is Kazakh, but Russian language remains the primary language of communication.

In 1991, the Soviet Union was dissolved by the agreement of the leaders of Russia, Ukraine, and Belarus[4]. As a result, in December 1991, the former Soviet Republics became independent states, and formerly internal borders became external. Among the 15 republics that constituted the former Soviet Union, 11 republics officially signed the Alma-Ata Protocols, signifying the formation of the Commonwealth of Independent States (CIS). Those were Azerbaijan, Armenia, Belarus, Kazakhstan, Kyrgyzstan, Moldova, Russia, Tajikistan, Turkmenistan, Uzbekistan and Ukraine. Georgia joined the organization in December 1993 (and later withdrew), whereas the Baltic States, namely Estonia, Latvia and Lithuania, chose not to participate in the formation of the CIS. The latter group of countries would soon be admitted to the European Union (2004), following very rapid economic and social reforms. The rest of the former Soviet Union, however, experienced significant stagnation in economic, political, and social development for several years (Blinnikov 2011).

The collapse of one of the largest and most powerful nations in the world, the Soviet Union, came at a significant cost to the former Soviet republics. Particularly, the Soviet Union had a unified

---

[3] For instance, in August 1937, Stalin issued an order to his aide, Molotov, to remove all Korean families, with no exception, from the Far Eastern region of the Soviet Union. Within a short timeframe, all Koreans were displaced and moved to the Central Asian republics including Kazakhstan. Koreans were rehabilitated after Stalin's death, and the details of this shameful historical process were released to the public only in the 1990s, after the collapse of the Soviet Union. Many other minority groups went through a similar repressions process and ended up in Kazakhstan. The author of this book has Korean grandparents who were a part of this repressions process and who were forced to leave the Far East in 1937.

[4] The Soviet period started in October 1917 with the victory of the Bolshevik party. It ended in August 1991 as a result of the Communist leaders' coup against Mikhail Gorbachev (see Blinnikov 2011). On December 8, 1991 in Belovezhskaja Puscha, the leaders of Ukraine, Russia and Belarus issued a statement that "The Soviet Union as a subject on international law and as a geopolitical reality ceased to exist" (Ayagan et al. 2011).

network of the natural gas and oil pipelines, centralized telecommunication and railroad systems, and a uniform national grid network (Blinnikov 2011). After 1991, not only did each state have to create a national security system at its border from scratch, but also had to make a challenging decision as to whether or not to quit this common system or to replace some elements of the old system with new ones, for which significant resources were required. Despite newly emerged geographical borders, all former Soviet republics remained heavily dependent on each other economically. In fact, the resource extracting industry was spread across the CIS states and it was unclear how to break down the previously unified system of mass production into pieces at least possible costs. Overall, an abrupt dissolution of the Soviet Union created chaos in economic and social spheres among the CIS nations for many years ahead.

Within the centrally planned Soviet Union system, Kazakhstan played a vital industrial role due to its enormous supplies of fossil fuels. Kazakhstan has been an oil producer since as early as 1911 and has had the second largest reserves after Russia (LOC, CIA 2013). The Soviet Union's program to industrialize the Central Asian region allowed building important transportation routes from Kazakhstan's remote coal, oil and gas fields to the European territories. This, however, left Kazakhstan with a mixed legacy after the collapse of the Soviet Union, as the efficiency of the energy industry heavily depended on the infrastructure that spread across other CIS nations and over which Kazakhstan no longer had control (LOC, CIA 2013). Being a landlocked nation, Kazakhstan had no access to sea ports and had to heavily rely on the pipelines system to transport the fossil fuels to the world's major markets.

The central role in the CIS reforms in the early 1990s belonged to Russia due to the fact that historically, major economic operations were governed from Moscow. The theory suggests two approaches regarding the formation of the free market economy in previously closed states: gradualism and a shock therapy (Melloni 2006). The leader of the Russian Federation, Boris Yeltsin, chose the latter approach, with the assistance of the foreign advisors[5]. During the period of 1991–1998 Russia was struggling to overcome the overwhelming effects of the two reforms launched by the first post-Soviet government of Russia that were part of the shocking therapy approach—(1) liberalization of prices to promote free competition, and (2) privatization of formerly owned enterprises (Blinnikov 2011). As a result of the first reform, within a few weeks commodity prices quadrupled, and by the end of 1992 the inflation rate reached 1,000 percent, remaining high over the next years (Worldwide Inflation Data 2012). At the same time, the economic output gradually declined and the population was unable to cope with rising prices, as income was not adjusted accordingly. As a result of the second, privatization reform, the ownership was highly concentrated in the hands of certain wealthy groups—oligarchs— and the general public did not get a stake in state enterprises[6].

Alongside the process of privatization and political reforms, in the 1990s the national government of Russia kept promoting the idea of investing in governmental securities called GKO bonds. Given the high yield offered on the bonds, the investments by the Russian population and foreign investors were rapidly growing. In reality, however, Russia was experiencing an overall economic and social downturn, a high level of inflation, and political instability. As such, the GKOs were not supported by the real economic growth and the only possibility to keep investors from withdrawing their funds was to steadily increase the yield (Melloni 2006). In June

---

[5] An example of the gradualism approach would be economic reforms in China that began in the 1970s and were arguably significantly less painful than those in the former Soviet Union (Melloni 2006). A well-known economist, Joseph Stiglitz, argues against the shocking therapy, suggesting that rapid privatization reforms, absent market competition, would have a negative impact on the economy.

[6] Blinnikov (2011) discusses the nature of the privatization process and the various schemes adopted in early 1990s in Russia. He suggests that this process was dominated by "grey" schemes that lacked transparency and left the major part of the population out of the process. A new class of rich individuals, oligarchs, emerged as a result of this process and the business structures ended up concentrated in the hands of a limited number of individuals. The privatization process in Kazakhstan resembled that in Russia.

1996 the yield reached 108 percent and by the end of the same year it dropped to just 36 percent. In August 1998 the Russian government defaulted on its GKO obligations. The result of the 1998 crisis was loss of credibility towards Russia within the global investment community and a massive outflow of investments.

The previously described processes in Russia that followed the collapse of the Soviet Union closely paralleled those in Kazakhstan. After declaring independence in 1991, Kazakhstan retained the basic political and governmental structure, and the former first secretary of the Communist Party of Kazakhstan, Nursultan Nazarbaev, was elected the president of the republic of Kazakhstan.

The first period of economic reforms in Kazakhstan covers 1991–1994, from declaration of independence until introduction of its national currency. The main feature of this period was that Kazakhstan remained in the Russian Ruble zone, implying that Kazakhstan heavily depended on the macroeconomic and monetary policies implemented within Russia (Berentaev 2001). Under heavy pressure from the Russian government, in January 1992 Kazakhstan declared liberalization of commodity prices that had a detrimental effect on the national economy. Particularly, Kazakhstan experienced hyperinflation in 1992–1998 that reached 2,000–3,000 percent in some years. The resource extraction industry that was the core of the national economy experienced a significant 60 percent decline in the output during the early 1990s (Kurganbayeva 2009). By 1994, about 70 percent of the population of Kazakhstan lived below the poverty line and workers did not receive salaries for months at a time (Kurganbayeva 2009). The privatization process in Kazakhstan was similar to that in Russia and began in 1992 with the sale of small and medium sized businesses. During the first year, 6,200 organizations were privatized (Berentaev 2001). In 1994, Kazakhstan started a mass privatization program, for which vouchers were distributed among the general population. During

1992–1995, about 15,000 organizations were privatized via different schemes that closely resembled those in Russia[7].

The second period of the economic reforms in Kazakhstan (1994–1997) is characterized by introduction of the national currency, Tenge, in 1993 following the decree of the President "Introducing the national currency of Republic of Kazakhstan" (National Bank of Kazakhstan 2016). Introduction of the currency allowed Kazakhstan to launch its own macroeconomic program, therefore reducing Kazakhstan's dependence on Russia. Nevertheless, experts noted an indirect influence of Russia in that the majority of economic reforms mirrored those of Russia during this period. More importantly, the international donor organizations, including the IMF and the World Bank, partly dictated the macroeconomic policies implemented by the Kazakhstani government (Berentaev 2001). The Tenge exchange rate against the US dollar was highly unstable upon introduction, declining from 5 to 56 Tenge per 1 USD within a few months (Ayagan et al. 2011). With the assistance of IMF, the national government of Kazakhstan was able to take control over the inflation processes and also stabilize the exchange rate for Tenge.

By 1997, it became evident that Kazakhstan's industrial output constituted only 21 percent of the Gross Domestic Product (GDP) and that the level of inflation was still high. About one million people (out of the total population of 17 million) were unemployed, and businesses reported the highest salary payment debts since the collapse of the Soviet Union (Kurganbayeva 2009). As a result, Kazakhstan experienced a massive migration of population to the nearby CIS states, primarily Russia. The Asian and the Russian crises in 1998 had a contagion effect on other economies, including that of Kazakhstan. The national currencies of the CIS countries were devalued, resulting in the loss of competitiveness for Kazakhstan's goods and the increase in import volumes. The National Bank

---

[7] The legal foundation for the process of privatization in Kazakhstan was provided by the law "On denationalization and privatization" (1991) and additionally, the law "On privatization" (1995) (Ayagan et al. 2011).

of Kazakhstan artificially maintained the Tenge exchange rate, spending roughly 1 billion USD. This led to significant decline in the country's gold reserves, and the Tenge was eventually devalued in April 1999.

Arguably, the period of 1997–1998 was a turning point for Kazakhstan. The national government established a long-term strategic plan of economic development of Kazakhstan until the year 2030, known as "Kazakhstan 2030", and the implementation of this important initiative started as early as in 1999 (Nazarbayev 1997). The main goal of the "2030" plan was formation of a competitive market economy, and the main priorities were placed on the development of innovation technologies, reduction of resource interdependence with other CIS states, and revival of the scientific base (Morozov 2005). By 2006, Kazakhstan was expected to join the pool of 50 most competitive economies in the world (Kurganbayeva 2009).

As a result of the radical reforms described herein, by 2000, Kazakhstan was the first CIS nation to reach an output production level comparable to that which existed immediately prior to the collapse of the Soviet Union. On average, during the period of 2000–2009, the growth rate of the national economy of Kazakhstan was about 9 percent, which is significantly higher than that of the country's main allies—Russia, Belarus and Ukraine (Kurganbayeva 2009). Importantly, the structure of the economy of Kazakhstan also experienced significant changes: by 2009, the industrial output contributed 44.4 percent, whereas the share of the service industry reached 54 percent. This suggests that overall, the economy of Kazakhstan became more diverse and balanced.

According to Blinnikov (2011), by 2008, Kazakhstan was by far the largest economy in Central Asia. The country had a vast natural resource base and successfully developed industrial sector, including the steel and nonferrous metallurgy, machinery, and oil and gas extraction. The world's sixth largest oil field, Tengiz, is based in the western part of the country. Russia remains the largest trade partner of Kazakhstan, receiving 12 percent of its exports (Blinnikov 2011). A distinctive feature of Kazakhstan's economic program was that it invited foreign oil companies to participate in oil and natural gas extraction. Particularly, about 80 percent of the country's petroleum is produced by Western companies. The development of the two major oil fields, Tengiz and Karachaganak, became possible mainly due to innovative extraction technologies brought about by international oil companies (LOC, CIA 2013). In 2008, the country's GDP per capita was the second largest after Russia, among all the CIS nations. Moreover, Kazakhstan had the highest exports of goods as a percentage of GDP, within the CIS.

In early 2008, the global financial crisis slowed down the economy of Kazakhstan and the country experienced a significant loss of capital inflows, resulting in a credit crunch (LOC, CIA 2013). The sharp drop in oil and commodity prices and the overall economic stagnation sent Kazakhstan into recession in 2009. Nevertheless, Kazakhstan rebounded fairly quickly: the GDP was on the rise again starting in 2010 and the growing commodity prices made a positive contribution towards the recovery process. The government realized that the overreliance of the national economy on oil and gas made it very vulnerable to global processes. Therefore, it established an ambitious diversification program aimed at developing other sectors of the national economy, including pharmaceuticals, telecommunication, and food processing (LOC, CIA 2013). In order to further increase the inflow of FDIs, Kazakhstan joined the Custom Union with Russia and Belarus, which is expected to improve trade relationship among the three nations.

Table 1 reports the data on the GDP volumes, as well as percentage changes, for Russia and Kazakhstan beginning in 1995, when the first wave of economic reforms was complete, until 2011. The statistics show that the average annual growth in total GDP was somewhat larger in the case of Russia, compared to Kazakhstan (33 versus 31 percent), whereas the average annual growth in GDP per capita was higher in the case of Kazakhstan (5 versus 4 percent). Unreported results show that these dynamics remain unchanged when the examined time period is split between the pre-1998 (pre-crisis) and post-1998 period.

Table 1. GDP and GDP per capita for Kazakhstan and Russia over 1995–2011.

Kazakhstan	1995	1996	1997	1998	1999	2000	2001	2002	2003	2004	2005	2006	2007	2008	2009	2010	2011	Ave. annual growth
GDP, current prices, national currency (billions)	1,014	1,416	1,672	1,733	2,016	2,600	3,251	3,776	4,612	5,870	7,591	10,214	12,850	16,053	17,008	23,008	29,380	
GDP growth	140%	40%	18%	4%	16%	29%	25%	16%	22%	27%	29%	35%	26%	25%	6%	35%	28%	31%
GDP per capita, constant prices, national currency (units)	24,783	25,225	26,126	26,024	26,834	29,535	33,554	36,804	40,000	43,480	47,245	51,704	55,688	56,695	55,877	59,070	62,586	
GDP per capita growth	-8%	2%	4%	0%	3%	10%	14%	10%	9%	9%	9%	9%	8%	2%	-1%	6%	6%	5%
Russia																		
GDP, current prices, national currency (billions)	1,429	2,008	2,343	2,630	4,823	7,306	8,944	10,819	13,208	17,027	21,610	26,917	33,248	41,277	38,809	45,166	54,369	
GDP growth	134%	41%	17%	12%	83%	51%	22%	21%	22%	29%	27%	25%	24%	24%	-6%	16%	20%	33%

GDP per capita, constant prices, national currency (units)	154,629	149,352	151,620	143,808	153,566	169,686	179,182	188,459	203,249	218,847	233,967	254,111	276,188	290,887	268,197	277,772	290,711
GDP per capita growth	-4%	-3%	2%	-5%	7%	10%	6%	5%	8%	8%	7%	9%	9%	5%	-8%	4%	5%	**4%**

Note: The table reports the absolute value and the percentage changes in GDP and GDP per capita for Kazakhstan and Russia, based on the statistics provided by the World Economic Outlook (IMF), Agency of Statistics of the Republic of Kazakhstan, and Federal State Statistics Services of Russia (2016).

According to the World Bank (2013) and the International Monetary Fund (2013), Kazakhstan has remained the strongest economy in the Central Asia region in terms of total economy growth and the inflow of investments. Notably, Kazakhstan was ahead of other CIS nations, including Russia, to repay the external debt to the IMF, and this was done 7 years ahead of schedule (The US Department of State 2015). While considerable amount of research attention has been devoted to Russia, among all CIS nations, it was Kazakhstan that attracted the highest FDI per capita and was able to withstand the recent economic slowdown with the least severe impact on the national economy (US Department of State 2015). According to the National Bank of Kazakhstan (2015), the country was the first nation in the CIS region to receive an investment grade from a major rating agency, Moody's, in 2002.

Table 2 reports the statistics on the dynamics of changes in total exports, expressed in USD, for Russia and Kazakhstan beginning in 1999 (post-crisis period) and until 2015. The average annual growth rate in the volume of total exports was higher in the case of Kazakhstan, compared to Russia (18 versus 12 percent, respectively). Figure 1 (upper picture) reports that Kazakhstan's growth in the GDP per capita exceeded that of the CIS over the period of 1992–2014. Figure 1 (lower picture) also shows that as of 2014, Kazakhstan's global competitiveness was higher than that of other CIS states, particularly in the areas such as macroeconomic environment, labor market efficiency, strength of regulatory institutions, and the market size.

Table 3 presents the most recent comparative statistics on various competitiveness indicators for Kazakhstan and Russia. Remarkably, Kazakhstan is ranked higher on a number of characteristics, including goods and labor market efficiency, macroeconomic environment, and strength of financial institutions, compared to Russia (World Economic Forum 2016). This evidence suggests that the course of fundamental economic reforms discussed above had a significant positive outcome. Nevertheless, Kazakhstan's stage of development is still defined as between the "factor driven" and the "efficiency driven", despite all the progress, and it has yet to reach the "innovation driven" stage that some emerging markets achieved years ago (United Arab Emirates, Qatar, etc.).

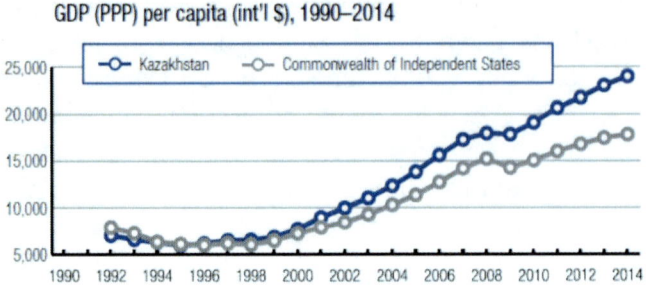

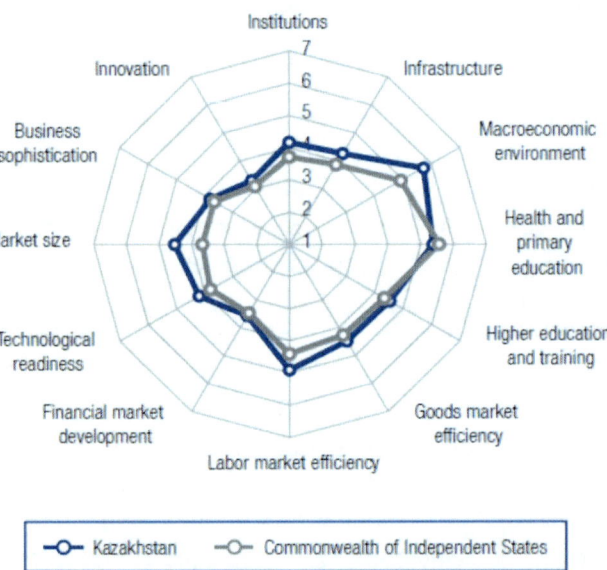

Figure 1. Upper picture: GDP per capita growth, Kazakhstan versus CIS. 1992–2014. Lower picture: Global competitiveness of Kazakhstan compared to other CIS states. Source: World Economic Forum 2016.

As of 2016, Kazakhstan is ranked at an all-time high in investor confidence and awareness, according to an Ernst & Young survey (2016). The recent admittance of Kazakhstan to the World Trade Organization (WTO) further enhances the potential of the country to attract higher FDIs. Arguably, Kazakhstan's reliance on external resources is the highest among the CIS countries, which explains the bundle of progressive policies adopted by the country's national government to attract foreign investment (World Bank 2015). These policies include reforms in the banking sector and pension system, changes in the tax laws and, most importantly, the devotion of significant resources to the development of the capital market system. The latter reforms entail commitment to transparent reporting and adoption of high quality accounting rules, such as International Financial Reporting Standards (IFRS), which is the focus of discussion in the next chapters.

Table 2. Total volume of exports and the export annual growth rate for Kazakhstan and Russia.

Kazakhstan	1999	2000	2001	2002	2003	2004	2005	2006	2007	2008	2009	2010	2011	2012	2013	2014	2015	Ave. annual growth
Total exports, million USD	5,592	9,140	8,647	9,665	12,900	20,093	27,851	38,250	47,755	71,184	43,196	59,971	84,336	86,449	84,700	79,460	45,726	
Growth	3%	63%	-5%	12%	33%	56%	39%	37%	25%	49%	-39%	39%	41%	3%	-2%	-6%	-42%	18%
Russia																		
Total exports, million USD	75,551	99,220	96,555	102,068	129,060	177,860	240,025	297,483	346,530	466,299	297,155	392,674	515,408	527,433	521,836	497,764	341,076	
Growth	1%	31%	-3%	6%	26%	38%	35%	24%	16%	35%	-36%	32%	31%	2%	-1%	-5%	-31%	12%

Note: The table reports the annual statistics on total exports (in millions USD) for Kazakhstan and Russia. Source: the World Economic Outlook (IMF), Agency of Statistics of the Republic of Kazakhstan, and Federal State Statistics Services of Russia (2016).

Table 3. Global Competitiveness Indicators for Kazakhstan and Russia (2015).

	Kazakhstan		Russia	
	Rank/140	score	Rank/140	score
Global Competitiveness Index Overall 1–7 (best)	42	4.5	45	4.4
Subindex A: Basic requirements 1–7 (best)	46	4.9	47	4.9
1st pillar: Institutions 1–7 (best)	50	4.2	100	3.5
2nd pillar: Infrastructure 1–7 (best)	58	4.2	35	4.8
3rd pillar: Macroeconomic environment 1–7 (best)	25	5.7	40	5.3
4th pillar: Health and primary education 1–7 (best)	93	5.4	56	5.9
Subindex B: Efficiency enhancers 1–7 (best)	45	4.4	40	4.5
5th pillar: Higher education and training 1–7 (best)	60	4.5	38	5
6th pillar: Goods market efficiency 1–7 (best)	49	4.5	92	4.2
7th pillar: Labor market efficiency 1–7 (best)	18	4.9	50	4.4
8th pillar: Financial market development 1–7 (best)	91	3.6	95	3.5
9th pillar: Technological readiness 1–7 (best)	61	4.2	60	4.2
10th pillar: Market size 1–7 (best)	46	4.5	6	5.9
Subindex C: Innovation and sophistication factors 1–7 (best)	78	3.5	76	3.5
11th pillar: Business sophistication 1–7 (best)	79	3.8	80	3.8
12th pillar: Innovation 1–7 (best)	72	3.3	68	3.3

Source: World Economic Forum (2016).

2.2. Capital market reforms and adoption of International Financial Reporting Standards (IFRS) in Kazakhstan

2.2.1. National stock market system

Capital markets, along with money markets, are the two core components of the financial market that brings together various parties—buyers and sellers—who are interested in trading with financial assets such as debt and equity instruments. Money markets are the markets where short-term instruments are traded, whereas capital markets are used principally for long-term trading with equity and debt instruments (Nasdaq 2016). Companies raise long-term equity-based funds primarily through issuance of share stocks in local and foreign capital markets, which is the focus of the discussion in this manuscript. Trades in money markets are predominantly executed among banks and other financial institutions via issuance of commercial papers and certificates of deposits, and this component of the financial market is not the main subject of this study and is not discussed further.

According to Goldman Sachs (2016), capital markets fuel nations' economic growth and their main purpose is to match the demand and supply for funds. Due to the process of globalization, as of 2013, emerging markets, including Kazakhstan and other CIS nations, reached an impressive third position in terms of the total market capitalization of trading assets, following the North American and the European Union regions (Goldman Sachs 2016). The degree of the maturity and the development progress of the capital market system directly impact individual nations and populations. A developed capital market system would encourage more companies to raise finance, therefore facilitating their growth, which would lead to creating new employment opportunities and promoting competition for new goods and services. Therefore, the capital market system is an essential component of any nation's economic development and prosperity. Not surprisingly, governments commit considerable resources to the development of the national capital market system.

The formation of the market economy in Kazakhstan started in the early 1990s in extremely difficult circumstances. The nation's leader, Nursultan Nazarbayev, was a supporter of the shocking therapy approach implemented within Russia, explaining the fact that the course of capital market reforms in Kazakhstan paralleled those in Russia. On one hand, transition to the market economy has had an unprecedented positive impact on Kazakhstan's development over time; on the other hand, it had spawned development of negative effects such as corruption, a shadow economy, and the like (Ayagan et al. 2011).

A national stock exchange, or a stock market, is the key component of any country's capital market system. The Kazakhstan Stock Exchange (KASE) was founded in 1993 and by 2013 this platform had become one of the most developed stock markets among the former Soviet Union countries (KPMG 2013). Formation of their own stock market in Kazakhstan followed introduction of the national currency, the Tenge, in 1993. Initially, KASE was designated as a currency trade platform, which explains its original name of Kazakhstan Inter-Bank Currency Exchange (KASE 2016). In 1995, the main shareholders of the exchange announced that KASE would become trading equity securities, for which the license was granted in October 1995 (KASE 2016). This license, however, only allowed the platform to execute trades with governmental securities. In 1996, the exchange was renamed as Kazakhstan Stock Exchange and received the unlimited license from the National Securities Commission of the Republic of Kazakhstan to trade various classes of securities (National Bank of Kazakhstan 2016). In 1997, KASE started trading with unlisted securities, and in 1999, the platform implemented the first transactions with corporate and municipal bonds.

Over the next several years, KASE underwent rapid development. Particularly, in 2002 the first trade of promissory notes was implemented; in 2003 the platform started trading with foreign government securities, and three years later, in 2006, with foreign corporate bonds (KASE 2016). In 2008, the exchange introduced its own Corporate Governance code with which public firms must comply and in 2010, KASE launched a progressive derivative market trading system. In 2011 KASE was recognized globally when it was included in the list of Dow Jones of the Federation of Euro-Asian Stock Exchanges, which comprises of the most prominent emerging markets with high potential (Dow Jones 2016). In the same year, several notable exchanges—Korea Exchange and Istanbul Stock Exchange—signed a memorandum of understanding and cooperation with KASE, therefore recognizing its status as one of the most progressive emerging stock markets. In 2013 KASE was admitted to the list of full members of the World Federation of Exchanges (World Federation of Exchanges 2016), and in the same year the Austrian Stock Exchange, Wiener Börse, developed a special stock market index for Kazakhstani companies, namely Kazakhstan Traded Index Local (Wiener Börse 2016). In 2014 KASE introduced the first trade in Chinese Yuan, therefore emphasizing the importance of the business relationships with one of its main traders, China, to the national economy.

Overall, in the past two decades, KASE was developing at a very impressive pace, which can be attributed to the strong governmental support and significant investments into the capital markets sphere. At present, KASE remains a joint-stock organization that has more than 40 major shareholders, including banks and national pension funds. The major shareholder that has an ownership of 50.1% is the National Bank of the Republic of Kazakhstan, which is also the main regulatory authority for the securities listing process in the country. Throughout its history, KASE has traded more than 200 governmental bonds issued by the Ministry of Finance and notes issued by the National Bank of Kazakhstan (National Bank of Kazakhstan 2016).

Datastream provides historical statistics regarding the global listing destinations of Kazakhstani public firms, as well as the origins of foreign firms listed in Kazakhstan. Historically, there have been 199 public companies that were affiliated with Kazakhstan. These firms were either Kazakhstani firms listed locally and/or overseas, or foreign firms listed in Kazakhstan, according to Datastream (2016). Table 4, column 1, reports that Kazakhstani firms actively pursued foreign listings, primarily in London and Germany, but also in Luxembourg, non-Nasdaq OTC, and other global platforms. These listings were in the form of common and preferred stock equities, debt instruments, and also American and Global Depositary Receipts (ADRs and GDRs, respectively). Table 4, column 3, shows that the majority of these public companies were incorporated in Kazakhstan, whereas several of them were registered in the United Kingdom, Australia and the United States. Kim (2013b) reported that CIS companies that are registered overseas (and are officially foreign firms) do so for tax benefits purposes and that they conduct their business predominantly within the CIS. The national legislature allows foreign issuers to be admitted to trade in the KASE. This evidence indicates that, although being relatively small, the Kazakhstani market is mildly integrated with the world's leading markets. The unreported results show that these 199 firms predominantly represent the extractive industry and the banking sector. As of May 2016, 80 of these companies maintained an active listing status (Datastream 2016).

Table 5 reports the changes in the market capitalization of domestic listed firms for Kazakhstan over the period of 2002–2014. Remarkably, there was an impressive growth in this metric until 2007, after which there was a significant decline in market capitalization in 2008 due to the global economic downturn discussed in the previous chapter. The most significant increase in the market capitalization of domestic listed firms occurred in 2005 and 2006 perhaps, not surprisingly, when Kazakhstan officially adopted IFRS (167 and 315 percent, respectively). From subsequent periods' data, it is evident that Kazakhstan's stock market has not fully recovered and the market capitalization as recorded at the end of 2014 has not even reached the pre-2008 crises level. The last two columns of Table 5 also show that the stock market liquidity dropped significantly in the last several years, when measured as a fraction of the GDP, and is far from the pre-crisis level. This evidence, however, is not unique to Kazakhstan. The Russian market, for instance, has experienced a similar decline in the stock market liquidity, although its recovery is going at a faster pace than that of Kazakhstani market. This can be explained by the greater maturity and depth of Russia's Moscow Exchange, compared to KASE, as well as greater internal financial resources (and lower external dependence) possessed by Russia.

As was noted previously, KASE underwent numerous reorganizational changes that made this platform an important player among all the emerging markets' exchanges. Nevertheless, critics suggest that the national government of Kazakhstan was not particularly successful at raising foreign investor attention towards the local public firms and KASE (KPMG 2013). At present, the foreign investor participation in KASE transactions remains at a very low level. Moreover, the numbers show that Kazakhstani local firms more increasingly prefer foreign markets, rather than KASE, when raising finance, due to their enhanced liquidity and greater investor pool. It therefore remains uncertain if Kazakhstan's stock market will show the same impressive growth as prior to the 2008 financial crisis, or if it will lose its positions to other global markets.

Table 4. Listing destinations and origins of public companies affiliated with Kazakhstan (Datastream).

Listing destinations of Kazakhstani firms	Number of firms	Origins of firms listed in Kazakhstan	Number of firms
KASE	155	Kazakhstan	188
London	10	United Kingdom	7
Xetra	10	Australia	2
Australian Stock Exchange (ASX)	1	United States	2
Berlin	2		
Deutsche Börse	9		
Luxembourg	4		
NewEx	2		
Non-Nasdaq OTC	5		
NYSE	1		
Total	**199**		**199**

Table 5. Market capitalization of domestic listed firms for Kazakhstan (Datastream).

Year	Market cap of domestic listed firms, USD	Change	As a % of GDP	Change
2002	1,289,440,000		5.23	
2003	2,425,900,000	88%	7.87	50%
2004	3,941,880,000	62%	9.13	16%
2005	10,528,660,000	167%	18.43	102%
2006	43,688,350,000	315%	53.93	193%
2007	41,377,500,000	-5%	39.46	-27%
2008	23,271,810,000	-44%	17.44	-56%
2009	27,929,370,000	20%	24.22	39%
2010	26,672,730,000	-4%	18.02	-26%
2011	22,537,310,000	-16%	11.98	-34%
2012	24,382,760,000	8%	11.65	-3%
2013	26,228,210,000	8%	11.31	-3%
2014	22,973,440,000	-12%	10.54	-7%

Interestingly, the process of the formation of the KASE and the structural changes in this stock market closely resembled those of the Russian stock exchanges, the Russian Trading System (RTS) and the Moscow Interbank Currency Exchange (MICEX). The MICEX was officially incorporated in 1992 and initially traded currencies, later becoming one of the most successful trading platform for equity instruments within Europe (World Federation of Exchanges 2016). The second platform, the RTS, was established in 1995 as the main equity trading platform and was modeled after the US's Nasdaq platform. The two exchanges, RTS and MICEX, were developing in parallel, until merging in 2011 into Moscow Exchange (see Kim 2013a, b). The KASE's model initially resembled that of MICEX and it only executed foreign currency exchange transactions. The main shareholder of Moscow Exchange is the Central Bank of Russia, whereas KASE's main shareholder is the National Bank of Kazakhstan. In 1995, when Russia's RTS was established as the official equity trading platform, KASE's shareholders also obtained the license to trade securities. Next, KASE's innovations including trades with derivative instruments and bonds were implemented shortly after they were introduced at RTS and MICEX. In 2012, when the unified Moscow Exchange developed its own clearing center using the European Clearstream and Euroclear systems, KASE also established a clearing department (KASE 2016, Moscow Exchange 2016). I elaborate on this parallelism in the next chapter when analyzing the capital markets reforms in Kazakhstan from the resource dependence perspective.

Nevertheless, at present, some notable differences between the Moscow Exchange and KASE exist. For example, in 2013, the Moscow Exchange expanded its line of services and introduced first trades with precious metals (gold and silver) and commodities (grain and other agricultural products). This innovation required a significant injection of investments and became possible due to the successful IPO conducted by the Moscow Exchange in 2012, which attracted foreign investors and was twice oversubscribed. Additionally, ownership of the Central Bank of Russia in the Moscow Exchange has dropped significantly, allowing expansion of the shareholder base that now includes foreign investors (Moscow Exchange 2016). It is unlikely, however, that similar innovations in KASE would have the same level of success, due to limited resources, and that KASE's activity would attract the same significant interest from foreign investors due to limited liquidity and stagnation in the pace of KASE's development in the past five years.

2.2. Adoption of International Financial Reporting Standards (IFRS) in Kazakhstan

As it will be extensively discussed in details in the next chapter, a successful push for mandating a universal set of accounting standards, namely IFRS, across the nations occurred around the turn of the twenty first century (Ball 2006). According to Ball (2006), one of the major pros of the global movement towards adoption of IFRS is an extraordinary reduction in the cost of communicating and transacting. Therefore, adopting a uniform set of accounting standards globally would lead to enhanced communication among market participants, resulting in increased integration among global markets (Ball 1995). The International Accounting Standards Board (IASB) that is based in London has done an extraordinary job at promoting the IFRS across nations, including emerging markets. Particularly, as of 2016, more than 120 nations not only expressed their endorsement of the global IFRS adoption process but actually committed to adoption of the IFRS on national levels.

The IFRS adoption literature extensively discussed the benefits to investors associated with a global adoption of IFRS. In his seminal study on pros and cons of IFRS, Ball (2006) suggests that among the direct benefits to investors are improved accuracy and timeliness of annual reports, reduced information processing costs, and enhanced comprehensiveness of reports for small investors and analysts, among others, which would facilitate the cross-border mergers and acquisitions and improve the flow of foreign direct investments (FDIs). These early predictions of Ball (2006) were supported recently by empirical studies. For example, Barth et al.

(2008, 2012) found that for a global sample of firms adopting IFRS, there has been significant improvement in reporting quality over time. Likewise, Christensen et al. (2013) reported that investors' reaction to the IFRS adoption event across nations was positive, on average. In a similar vein, Naranjo et al. (2016) documented that firms are more likely to raise external finance via equity issuance, as opposed to debt issuance, following an IFRS adoption event. Overall, prior literature is at consensus regarding the expectation that adoption of IFRS at a national level would facilitate investment flows, leading to growth in the national stock market system.

Despite the above noted benefits regarding the global adoption of IFRS, this process is initially very costly for countries, particularly emerging markets. Among the major costs associated with this process, Ball (2006) cites imperfections in the local political system, enhanced earnings management due to lack of enforcement, limitations of corporate laws and national tax legislatures, and lack of supporting infrastructure. Indeed, several studies documented that emerging nations were unsuccessful in their IFRS adoption efforts as a result of the above mentioned limitations and that firms did not experience a predicted improvement in reporting quality, therefore disappointing global investors and leading to outflow of investments (Karampinis and Hevas 2011). Clearly, a national government contemplates various advantages and disadvantages of this fundamental reform when making a decision about implementing it on a national level.

The very first attempt to introduce Western-style reporting practices in Kazakhstan dates back to 1995 when the government announced that national GAAP would be developed in the near future and that it would be based on International Accounting Standards (IAS), the predecessor of IFRS[8]. In 1996, the Kazakh GAAP were officially adopted. Beginning in 2005, all listed companies in the European Union's regulated markets had to prepare consolidated financial statements using IFRS. Arguably, this was one of the key events that pushed other global markets and even entire

---

8   IAS and IFRS are used interchangeably in this study.

regions to introduce IFRS into their reporting practices. Interestingly enough, Kazakhstani government made the IFRS adoption reporting a mandatory requirement for all banks and other financial institutions as early as in 2004. This was ahead of the IFRS adoption reforms implemented within the developed markets such as those of the EU, and also other emerging markets. This decision surprised the capital market participants but was the result of following the capital market reforms in Kazakhstan's closest ally—Russia— whose government also issued a requirement for banks to adopt IFRS in 2004, shortly before the Kazakhstani government issued a similar intention. In November 2004, the Russian government also declared plans to adopt IFRS for all categories of public firms. Although this initiative was initially approved by the Russian Duma (parliament), this plan was stalled until 2010 when it was finally approved, and in 2011, the Russian government officially signed on the IFRS adoption reform, requiring consolidated financial statements to be prepared starting in 2011 (see Kim 2013a, b). Therefore, Russia backed off from the initial plan to make the IFRS reporting mandatory for all categories of public firms.

Kazakhstan, nonetheless, decided to proceed with the IFRS adoption plans, notwithstanding Russia's actions, and beginning in 2005, IFRS were required for all listed companies, extractive industry companies, and those with significant governmental ownership. Since 2013, all state-owned enterprises are also required to prepare financials reports in accordance with IFRS. This event was unprecedented in many respects. First, Kazakhstan was significantly behind Russia in terms of the stage of the development of its capital market system and also maturity of its supporting infrastructure. Second, it was the first CIS nation to make a commitment to a fundamental change in the reporting practice of public firms. Accordingly, the global investment community expressed skepticism regarding the success of the implementation of this reform in Kazakhstan. For example, Tyrrall et al. (2007) suggested that this process would work against public firms and that the outcome of the IFRS adoption reform was unlikely to be positive.

What was the major driver behind Kazakhstan's decision to become an early and first adopter of IFRS within the CIS, pioneering one of the most fundamental changes in the reporting environment? I propose that it was the country's unprecedented need for foreign direct capital, in order to sustain its economic growth and the course of ongoing reforms, which prompted the national government to implement the IFRS adoption reform early and within a short timeframe. In chapter 4, I analyze Kazakhstan's strategic decision to adopt IFRS ahead of the Russian and other emerging markets using the resource dependence framework.

Chapter 3. Global adoption of IFRS

3.1. History behind the global movement to adopt a uniform set of accounting standards and the evolvement of IFRS

Despite the fact the IFRS gained popularity in 2005, the year in which regulated markets within the European Union made preparation of IFRS-based reports mandatory, the debate regarding the need for accounting harmonization began long before this date—circa 1960s. This debate was sparked by realization in the global community that lack of comparability in financial reports prevented capital flow and significantly impeded the efficiency of global capital allocation. Indeed, investors are better off investing in high performing companies, provided that their financials are transparent and can be understood. However, if informational barriers are substantial and investors bear unreasonably high costs of processing information then they would divert their capital to less efficient but more transparent companies. Companies located in the markets whose national accounting reports are difficult to interpret due to peculiarities of the national reporting requirements would inevitably be considered as more risky and would have higher cost of capital than their counterparts from more transparent markets. Harmonization of accounting standards, defined as reduction in differences in reporting rules and practices globally, would improve understandability and credibility of financial reports and facilitate cross-border financial transactions. This term and the process were first discussed by the International Accounting Standards Committee (IASC) that operated during 1973–2001 and was a predecessor of the nowadays International Accounting Standards Board (IASB) that is based in London (IASB 2016).

During the 1970s and 1980s, there were several directives issued within the EU that were aimed at harmonizing reporting practices across countries. Particularly, the Fourth Directive (1978) and the Seventh Directive (1983) were crucial to the EU's harmonization initiative. The former directive introduced the concept of the "true and fair view" that should be applied upon preparation of the balance sheet and income statement, whereas the latter concept established the requirements for preparation of consolidated financial statements (European Commission 1998, 2003). Although these two directives led to progressive changes in the reporting practices of the European companies, they allowed several alternatives to coexist, which essentially opened the door to non-comparability of the financial statements (Doupnik 1992). Joos and Lang (1994) examined reporting practices within the UK and Germany and concluded that the directives provided more form than substance due to differences in the main incentives and reporting models in the two countries (shareholder versus government oriented). The authors found no evidence of convergence in major ratios (PE, ROE, etc.) after implementation of the directives, suggesting that their introduction did not result in anticipated improvement in reporting practices.

In summary, not all were supportive of the harmonization idea. The opponents of this initiative claimed (not without merits, as time would show) that cross-country differences in legal, political, economic, and cultural environments would dominate the harmonization efforts and that developing nations would in fact suffer from this process, rather than benefit from it. Saudagaran (2009) among others, suggested that adopting Western-style global reporting practices would suppress the choices and the voice of the emerging markets, essentially making the harmonization process one form of colonialism. In addition, critics argued that investors already acted rationally and had a complete ability to analyze financial statements of global companies operating under varying sets of rules. Hence, there was no real need for adopting international reporting standards. Hoarau (1995) contended that the social function of accounting was lost in France, for example, under heavy influence of the harmonization efforts. The author also questioned the means of achieving harmonization and its consequences across the nations[9].

Despite its limitations, the process of harmonization left its foot print in history in that the sole idea of making financial statements comparable across nations was a novelty in the global reporting practices. Although this process was generally characterized as inefficient, as it allowed numerous reporting alternatives to co-exist as long as they did not conflict with each other, a more important process—*convergence* of accounting standards—grew out of the basic rationalities for harmonization. Convergence has a different meaning and, unlike harmonization, it implies adopting one set of accounting standards globally. Similar to harmonization, it takes place over time. The IASB's main goal is to achieve international convergence of accounting standards, for which it cooperates with national standard-setters across the world. The major efforts of IASB have been aimed at creating a high quality set of reporting rules and practices (IFRS Foundation Constitution 2013).

Since 2005, all companies listed on the EU-regulated markets were required to prepare consolidated reports under IFRS or another GAAP that were deemed equivalent. This requirement arises from EU regulation 1606/2002, which mandated the use of IFRS for listed groups. Prior to 2005, countries within the EU followed a variety of country-specific reporting rules. This event has had an unprecedented impact on global popularity of IFRS. Within a short timeframe, 100 nations started requiring or allowing IFRS for public companies, including small states and emerging markets (IAS Plus Deloitte 2006). A significant number of countries also committed to gradually converge their national accounting standards with IFRS. Importantly, since 2002, the IASB has worked closely with the US Financial Accounting Standards Board (FASB)

---

9 Another classic example that is commonly cited in the literature examining the impact of adoption of international standards is the case of Deutsche Bank of Germany (Saudagaran 2009). The company switched to US GAAP in 2002 in order to be able to raise finance on the NYSE. As a result, the company's profit under the local accounting standards turned into a loss under US GAAP, leaving investors and analysts confused and disappointed.

towards convergence of IFRS and US GAAP. Schipper (2005) identified the implications of the international convergence efforts and suggested that IASB would need to provide detailed implementation guidance post 2005 when the IFRS are mandated within the EU. Otherwise, firms and auditors would turn to other sources including US GAAP and home-country GAAP.

Another pivotal event that evidenced of global acceptance of IFRS as high quality reporting standards was elimination of the requirement for foreign issuers listed in the US to prepare reports in accordance with US GAAP. The Final Rule on acceptance of the IFRS financial statements from foreign issuers is formulated in the SEC's Release Nos. 33–8879; 34–57026; International Series Release No. 1306; File No. S7–13–07. According to the Rule, foreign private issuers are allowed to include in their filings with the SEC financial statements prepared in accordance with IFRS as issued by the IASB without reconciliation to US GAAP. The exemption from the reconciliation requirement relates to both annual and required interim reporting periods and applies to financial years ending after November 15, 2007. In summary, the uniform adoption of IFRS has been progressing at a very fast pace with an impressive degree of success[10].

In his seminal work that was published shortly after mandating IFRS within the EU, Ball (2006) outlined the major anticipated benefits of adoption of IFRS for investors. Particularly, IFRS adoption promises timely and more accurate financial reports to global investors, compared to local standards-based financials issued upon varying deadlines. Small investors will be in a better position to compete with large investors due to improved quality of financial statements and reduced information acquisition costs. Next, financial analysts will face lower cost of processing information and issue

---

[10] Deloitte reports the status of IFRS adoption by jurisdiction and IFRS development archive/news, which can be found at: http://www.iasplus.com/en/resources/ifrs-topics/use-of-ifrs. PWC also offers the summary of IFRS adoption by jurisdiction at: http://www.pwc.com/us/en/issues/ifrs-reporting/publications/ifrs-status-country.html.

more accurate forecasts, resulting in more efficient information dissemination and capital allocation. Companies can expect lower cost of capital as a result of a larger shareholding base and lower level of information asymmetry. Increased transparency would reduce agency conflicts, too. Ball (2006) also predicted improved cross-border flow of investment, the proposition that was empirically tested more recently. Prior studies documented that global convergences of accounting standards through adoption of IFRS is expected to decrease information processing costs, thus facilitating the inflow of Foreign Direct Investments (FDIs) and increasing the scope of cross-border mergers and acquisitions (Amiram 2012, Chen et al. 2014). This provide strong incentives for emerging markets, for example, to join the IFRS adoption pool.

Nevertheless, the success of IFRS adoption globally has not been uniform and many concerns were raised regarding the attributes that would make this process successful at a national level. Ball (2006) predicted that global adoption of IFRS will be overwhelmingly uneven around the world, including the EU itself that promulgated these standards. Thus, de jure adoption of IFRS will not necessarily lead to de facto uniform implementation of these standards. This is due to the fact, Ball argued, that IFRS adoption is foremost a political process, and that political and economic processes influence reporting practices on a local level. Differences in the degrees of enforcement, infrastructure, and legal environments would contribute towards uneven implementation of IFRS globally. Overall, Ball (2006) suggested there were valid reasons behind the skepticism regarding the success of global adoption of IFRS, as market forces (regulators, auditors, analysts, etc.) and politics are defined locally rather than globally. It is likely that managers and auditors would implement discretion over how the uniform rules such as IFRS are implemented, which would lead to uneven and deferred implementation of IFRS across regions. In a related study, La Porta et al. (1997) found that a country's financial system is affected by its legal origins that are correlated with the level of investor protection. The authors found that common law countries generally have better reporting systems, higher transparency, and enhanced investor protection, compared to code law countries.

3.2. Empirical evidence regarding implementation of IFRS: economic and legal explanations to the degree of success of IFRS adoption

Francis & Schipper (1999) define the value relevance of information as the ability of accounting numbers to explain investor returns and market prices. The empirical literature examined value relevance of book value and earnings long before voluntary and mandatory adoption of IFRS became a global trend. Originally, the studies primarily focused on cross-sectional settings whereby value relevance of accounting numbers was compared across countries or a group of countries. In particular, the *Code versus Common Law* partition of countries was popular in the empirical literature and was based on the expectation that information produced in the common law, investor oriented environment had superior value relevance when compared to information produced under the code law, stakeholder oriented system (e.g. Ball et al. 2000, Joos and Lang 1994). The explanation behind this pattern is that in common law countries, investor rights are emphasized and the legal system offers strong support to them, whereas in code law countries, there is less demand for information and banks are primary providers of finance. Ball et al. (2000) examined conservatism and timeliness for two groups of countries partitioned as common law (Australia, Canada, UK, and USA) and the code law (France, Germany, and Japan) nations. The examination period covered 1985–1995, which is long before the global IFRS convergence movement started. The findings of the study are that firms representing code law nations report earnings that are less timely and less conservative compared to earnings reported by firms from the common law countries.

A parallel debate vis-à-vis differential reporting quality was based on the *developed versus emerging market* partitioning of countries (Kim 2013a). This classification relies on the assumption that emerging markets are characterized by poor infrastructure, insufficient regulations, and market inefficiency, and their reporting practices are heavily influenced by local political forces. Therefore, companies domiciled in emerging markets are expected to report lower quality information, compared to their peers from developed markets (see Abdel-khalik et al. 1999, Kim 2013a). The process of transition to Western-style reporting practices was most pronounced in Eastern European countries, including CIS that were part of the Soviet Bloc prior to the 1990s. Solodchenko and Sucher (2005) identified the political problems of misalignment of interests between the accounting elite and the government when it comes to implementation of reforms in Ukraine. Kosmala (2005) examined application of the True and Fair View (TFV) concept (based on the IAS framework) in Poland and concludes that "in practice, there appears to be a lack of consensus in translation and grammatical construction of the TFV concept, revealing a general local unfamiliarity with the substance of this 'Western'-originated and constructed predominantly in the British and American context construct". Overall, transition of emerging markets towards the IAS/IFRS proved to be challenging.

Due to the global IFRS adoption trend discussed previously, there was a shift in motivation, and international accounting literature increasingly focused on benefits associated with *voluntary* and *mandatory* adoption of IFRS, compared to the local accounting standards. These studies generally fall into two categories: studies performing comparative analysis of changes in value-relevance of information over time for multi-country samples (Barth et al. 2008, 2012), and studies examining changes in value-relevance of information in the pre-post IFRS adoption period in one-country settings (Alali and Foote 2012, Bartov et al. 2005, Karampinis and Hevas, 2011, Kim 2016a, Prather-Kinsey 2006). Studies commonly examined changes in value relevance of earnings and book value per share, or changes (differences) in the degree of conditional conservatism and timeliness of reported information due to adoption of IFRS.

The findings of this IFRS adoption value relevance literature are largely mixed. Barth et al. (2008) focused on voluntary IFRS adopters representing 21 countries and found that value-relevance of earnings and timeliness of recognition of losses improved following adoption of IFRS. Bartov et al. (2005) examined comparative value relevance of earnings for German firms listed on the New Market and documented that this metric is higher under IAS and US GAAP, compared to the German GAAP; however, there was no difference in value relevance between the IAS and US GAAP-based earnings. In contrast, Hung and Subramanyam (2007) found very limited evidence of improvement in value relevance and conditional conservatism of earnings for the sample of German firms. The value relevance evidence of improvement in quality of reported information as a result of IFRS adoption in emerging markets is also mixed. Liu and Liu (2007) reported higher value-relevance of information for the B-shares listed on the Chinese market and reporting under IAS. Interestingly, for the same Chinese market, Chen et al. (2001) found no evidence of improved earnings quality for a sample of firms that were required to reconcile Chinese GAAP numbers to IAS. The more recent evidence of Karampinis and Hevas (2011) on Greece suggests that mandatory adoption of IFRS only marginally improves quality of accounting information. Ahmed et al. (2013) performed a meta-analysis of the IFRS adoption literature and found that value relevance of book value did not increase, whereas value relevance of earnings and accuracy of analyst forecasts generally improved post adoption of IFRS.

A related stream of literature examined the market reaction, changes in liquidity and cost of capital around the IFRS adoption event. For the sample of 26 countries, Daske et al. (2008) reported improvements in these metrics, but only based on the premises that the major effects occur before the switch to IFRS. In a follow up study, Daske et al. (2013) found that these capital market effects are statistically significant in the case of "serious" adopters, as opposed to the "label" adopters. Armstrong et al. (2012) documented an incrementally negative market reaction to several IFRS-related events in the case of the code law countries, compared to common law countries, suggesting that investors are concerned whether the benefits of IFRS adoption would materialize. In a more recent study, Olibe (2016) documented a positive market reaction to IFRS-based earnings reported by the UK firms cross-listed in the US. On the other hand, Kim (2016b) found that London-based investors reacted negatively to the IFRS adoption news in the case of the Russian firms, raising concerns over the de facto IFRS implementation path[11].

In summary, the predictions articulated by Ball (2006) found support in the empirical literature in that there was no general consensus regarding the IFRS adoption benefits in global settings. Among potential explanations for variations in IFRS adoption practices are differences in incentives of preparers of financial statements to comply with high quality reporting rules, the level of shareholder and investor protection, and efficiency of the institutional framework, among others (Ball 2006, Ball et al. 2003, Daske et al. 2008, La Porta et al. 1997, 2000). Those factors, individually or collectively, ultimately define the quality of financial statements and the properties of accounting numbers, the studies concluded.

3.3. Alternative explanations to the IFRS adoption consequences, not limited by legal and economic arguments. Evidence regarding the IFRS adoption benefits for CIS countries

In the most recent study, Ramanna and Sletten (2016) take a different perspective, not limited by political, legal and economic explanations proposed by Ball (2006), on the perceived IFRS adoption benefits on the national level. The authors rely on the economic theory of networks to predict nations' shifts away from local accounting

---

11 Weetman (2005) discusses the challenges associated with reconciling and comparing the results of various IFRS-based studies, as empirical works are typically based on different samples subject to various degrees of data availability. This was an important issue, particularly in earlier IFRS-related literature when databases had limited coverage of emerging markets.

standards towards IFRS during the period of 2003–2008. They found that the more countries adopt IFRS, the greater the net perceived informational benefits to the network of countries using IFRS. Smaller countries and those that have ties with the EU, the authors argue, benefit more from the increase in network benefits and are more likely to surrender their national accounting standards in favor of IFRS. Next, studies examining the association between the level of investor protection and the IFRS adoption perspective found that less developed countries are more likely to adopt IFRS and surrender to international reporting standard settings organizations (Hope et al. 2006). This phenomenon can be best explained by the *bonding* perspective: when adopting IFRS, countries effectively signal their commitment to transparent reporting and enhanced investor protection (see Coffee 1999, Stulz 1999).

Further, recent empirical works adopted novel, complementary frameworks, grounded in the *institutional* theory of sociology. Based on the sample of 71 countries, Alon and Dwyer (2014) reported that under a wide array of external isomorphic pressures and conditional on the degree of resource dependency, countries choose a specific IFRS adoption strategy—to require, permit, or not allow IFRS. Judge et al. (2010) reported that external institutional pressures were indicative of nations' decisions to adopt IFRS, based on the sample of 132 nations with different origins and IFRS adoption strategies. By adopting IFRS, the authors propose, countries signal their participation in the legitimate global models[12]. Cannizzaro and Weiner (2015) documented that societal expectations dominate agency-theory motivations, such as securing external finance, in determining the scope of disclosure and transparency in the case of multinational firms. The significance of societal pressures in corporate reporting practices was also highlighted in Hope (2003) and Salter et al. (2013).

Using unique Russian settings, Kim (2016a) applied the neo-institutional framework of DiMaggio and Powell (1983) to explain

---

12 See also Guerreiro et al. (2012), Hassan et al. (2014), Rodrigues and Craig (2006), and Touron (2005).

the differential changes in reporting quality post adoption of IFRS for several categories of Russian public firms, such as mandatory IFRS adopters, blue chips, and non-adopters. The author reports that the external institutional pressures are not necessarily predictive of the country's IFRS adoption success and firms' strategic responses to this reform. Rather, internal isomorphic pressures shape differential consequences of IFRS adoption for various categories of public firms.

The reporting reforms, including adoption of IFRS in Kazakhstan and other CIS countries, received limited attention. Studies were primarily implemented in relation to the 1990s when the accounting reforms began but were going at a very slow pace. Smirnova et al. (1995) analysed changes in the accounting training during the transition period within Russia, while Bychkova (1996) and Sucher and Bychkova (2001) described the changes in internal and external auditing practices during the 1990s. Sokolov and Kovalev (1996) focused on the challenges faced by the accounting profession after 1991, following the collapse of the Soviet Union. Bourmistrov and Mellemvik (1999) analysed the evolution of accountancy in Russia's local governments. Goncharov and Zimmermann (2006) examined the earnings management behavior of Russian companies in 2001–2002. The authors found that firms had propensity to manage earnings downward to reduce income tax payments, and this strategy was more prevalent among private firms that had less incentives to provide high quality reports, compared to public firms. Richard (1995) examined changes in Russia's and Romania's reporting practices in the early 1990s and concluded that the fall of the Soviet Union did not lead to adoption of Anglo-American reporting formats and that Russian firms still produced reports in reference to an old standardized chart of accounts.

Alon (2013) examined factors that affect firms' perceptions of the adoption of IFRS within the context of co-existence of the local standards with IFRS. For the sample of blue chips exclusively and based on the period of 1995–2010, Kim (2013a) showed that information provided under IFRS-based reports was more value relevant than that prepared under RAS. In the most recent study, Kim

(2016a) shows that Russian public firms that experienced *coercive*, *mimetic* and *normative* societal pressures—those that both adopted IFRS and were affected by other regulatory reforms—experienced significant improvements in reporting quality. The author does not find such evidence for firms that experienced only *coercive* pressure—those that were affected by changes in regulations but were exempt from the IFRS reporting requirement. Based on this evidence, Kim (2016a) concludes that the IFRS adoption reform had an incrementally positive contribution towards improvement in reporting quality of Russian public firms, over the effect of other regulations that were implemented contemporaneously with IFRS adoption.

To my knowledge, the only study that examines the relevance of the IFRS adoption reform to Kazakhstan is that of Tyrrall et al. (2007). The authors analyzed changes in the reporting environment during the period of 1991–2006 and concluded that Kazakhstan had no choice but to proceed with adoption of IFRS. The major findings from this study are that IFRS would take pace slowly and the eventual success of this reform was somewhat uncertain, due to the limited resources of the country and the recent communist past. The study of Tyrrall (2007), however, does not provide empirical evidence regarding the economic consequences of this reform, which would be of significant importance to global investors and standard setters from other emerging economies. This manuscript attempts to fill this gap.

Chapter 4. Resource dependence theory and its application to Kazakhstan's strategic decision to become the first and early adopter of IFRS within the CIS

4.1. The main provisions of the Resource Dependence Theory

In this section, I describe the main provisions of the resource dependence theory pioneered by Pfeffer and Salancik (1978). This is the framework that I rely on to analyze Kazakhstan's strategic decision to become the first adopter of IFRS within the CIS. I use individual CIS countries as the local unit of analysis and the global investment community (international donors, foreign governments, unions) represents larger social networks in my analysis, whereas in the original study of Pfeffer and Salancik (1978) organizations are the basic units of analysis and the national governments are high level social actors.

In 1978, Pfeffer and Salancik published a book, "The external control of organizations: A resource dependence perspective", that subsequently became a pivotal work. In this work, the authors propose the resource dependence theory (hereafter, RDT) to explain how organizations reduce their environmental interdependencies and uncertainty. The RTD has become one of the most influential frameworks, predominantly in organizational and management studies. More recently, this theory has been applied as a major framework to a variety of other topics across a wide range of disciplines, which will be discussed next.

According to Pfeffer and Salancik (1978), organizations operate under the influence of pressures from various external groups, and managers' actions are aimed at reducing environmental uncertainties and interdependence with other organizations. Pfeffer (1987) notes that these two factors lead to a situation where survival and success of an organization are uncertain. Managing resource interdependence, however, is not always successful and can produce other forms of dependence, which in turn will have influence on an organization's behavior. Pfeffer and Salancik (1978) suggest that firms can take five actions in order to minimize resource interdependence and attain more power: [1] participate in mergers and acquisitions, [2] form joint ventures and other types of alliances, [3] manage size, composition, and other attributes of the board of directors, [4] implement executive succession, and [5] participate in a political action. Each of these alternative routes and the related empirical evidence are discussed next.

In the past three decades, the RDT has become the dominant theory explaining rationales behind firms' mergers and acquisitions (M&A) strategies (Hillman et al. 2009). Pfeffer and Salancik (1978, chapter 6) suggest that vertical or horizontal integration represents an effective method of extending organizational control over others, attaining dominance to increase the power in exchange relationships, and decreasing dependence on other, dominant organizations (p. 114). Empirical studies generally found support to the above proposition. Pfeffer (1972) reported that firms often use the M&A strategies to reduce direct market competition. Likewise, Walter and Barney (1990) suggested that managers attempt to reduce firm dependence within the same business environment by engaging in M&A activities. On the other hand, some empirical studies suggest that resource interdependence may not be the sole factor in the M&A process. Factors such as institutional norms, industry environment, and various internal considerations are equally important in explaining managerial choice to engage in the M&A activities (Palmer and Barber 2001, Hitt and Tyler 1991, among others). More recently, the study of Casciaro and Piskorski (2005) provides important refinements to the original RDT of Pfeffer and Salancik (1978). Particularly, the authors highlight the different dimensions of the interdependence and propose that mutual dependencies increase the scope of M&A, while the power imbalance restrains them.

Second, the RDT also suggests an alternative mechanism to manage interdependencies—by forming joint ventures and other inter organizational relationships such as strategic alliances and buyer-supplier networks. These methods of reducing external dependencies and environmental uncertainty are different from the M&A strategy discussed previously. First, they do not assume complete absorption, as in the case of mergers, and second, these cooperative mechanisms are typically occasional and can be short-lived (Pfeffer and Salancik 1978, chapter 7). Next, M&A transactions are not always possible when there are many small competitors. In this case business or professional associations, alliances, and joint ventures represent a more effective power coordinating mechanism (p. 144). Empirical research found support to the RDT's application to joint ventures. Stearns et al. (1987) and Elg (2000), among others, found that various forms of inter organizational relationships are used by firms to reduce environmental complexity. Das et al. (1998) reported that smaller firms typically benefit more from cooperative alliances. The RDT was successfully integrated with the game theory, agency theory, and economic theory of networks, for instance. Like the M&A application discussed herein, more recently the RDT's application to joint ventures was refined. Lomi and Pattison (2006) propose that inter organizational dependencies exist across multiple networks and are therefore not local. As an extension to the RDT, Gulati and Sytch (2007) point to the difference between the strategies involving joint dependence and dependence asymmetry, which may have different incentives and outcomes.

Next, the RDT theory found its application in the corporate governance studies that examined the impact of the composition of a board of directors on firm performance. The dominating theory in this field is the agency theory; however, the RDT has had a great influence on the empirical research in this area, too. In fact, some studies suggest that the RDT provides a more useful perspective to examine the role of a board of directors in firms' decision making processes (Hillman et al. 2009). Pfeffer (1972) argued that board composition and size are firms' rational responses to external environmental pressures. In their meta-analysis study, Dalton et al. (1999) found that generally there is a positive association between board size and firm performance. Other studies, however, argued that this relationship is not as straightforward and that prior performance and a firm's strategy are the two major determinants of the board composition (Pearce and Zahra 1992). Pfeffer and Salancik (1978, chapter 7) propose that there are various benefits brought by directors to an organization, including expertise and advice, unique information, access to additional resources, and legitimacy. The research studies found that these attributes are particularly important for early development firms and regulated industries and that they have a positive impact on social and corporate performance of firms (Johnson and Green 1999). Importantly, boards of directors bring in supplemental, marginally significant resources that the management does not have, which explains why firms value directors who are former politicians (Lester et al. 2008). Overall, the empirical research generally supports the RDT's assertion that board composition, size and expertise help firms manage their environmental interdependencies and uncertainties, allowing them to attain more power.

Further, Pfeffer and Salancik (1978) propose that organizations can successfully cope with environmental uncertainty by using an executive succession mechanism. The selection and removal of executives can help organizations achieve better alignment with their environments (p. 299). This is so because any visible failures of an organization are inevitably driven by failure of those who are in charge and their poor expertise (p. 236). This proposition found strong support in the empirical studies. For example, Harrison et al. (1988) reported that an increased rate of executives' turnover pertains to firms that are more dependent on their environments. Other studies documented that firms are more likely to replace their CEOs following the period of poor financial performance and that market participants react favorably to this event (Zhang 2006). Additionally, greater environmental uncertainty manifests in shorter tenure for executives. Moreover, empirical studies documented that the selection of an outside or an inside candidate for top management positions depends on the performance of an organization (Dalton and Kesner 1983), and a probability of hiring an external candidate increases with a degree of financial distress (Schwarz and Menon 1985). Overall, empirical literature consistently found support to the notion that the degree of the interdependence and environmental uncertainty affects the tenure and turnover rate of executives.

4.2. Application of the Resource Dependence Theory to Kazakhstan's strategic decision to become the first adopter of IFRS within the CIS

Lastly and most importantly, Pfeffer and Salancik (1978) propose that organizations can manage interdependencies and environmental uncertainties through political actions (chapter 8). Hillman et al. (2009) argue that this application of the RDT has received limited attention in organization studies, compared to the four areas discussed previously. The chapter 8 of Pfeffer and Salancik's seminal work, "The created environment: controlling interdependencies through laws and social actions", has a direct application to this study. The authors suggest that while organizations may influence local pressures (on a firm level), they rarely have control over actions of larger social players such as national governments. For example, in heavily regulated industries (airlines, extractive industries) companies are under heavy pressure from the governmental agencies that prohibit certain actions such as diversification of resources into alternative businesses or elimination of the entire lines of business that are unprofitable (p. 189). None of the previously discussed strategies such as M&A, creating alliances, etc. represent successful mechanisms to manage external resource dependence, as there are always higher level pressures and uncertainties that remain unresolved.

The above provisions of the RDT directly apply to the situation within the CIS in the early 1990s. In the case of Kazakhstan and other CIS nations, after the collapse of the Soviet Union, managing economic uncertainties while trying to build a Western-style capital market system with the use of local resources had limited success, as was noted in the previous chapters. First, each CIS nation experienced significant budget deficit and extremely low levels of the national output, and second, each country gradually became a part of several global networks managed by international organizations and unions, over which they had no control. Immediately after gaining independence, Kazakhstani government attempted to build a new economic system through cooperation with other CIS states, the major of which was the Russian Federation. An example of such cooperation was mutual bilateral agreements regarding import-export trade relationships and the parallelism in the capital market and economic reforms that were extensively discussed in this manuscript. The RDT would suggest that this cooperative mode and parallelism in reforms was because Kazakhstan and Russia faced similar environmental interdependencies due to being the largest trading partner of the other after dissolution of the Soviet Union. Indeed, Mullery et al. (1995) documented similar patterns of political campaigns contributions by firms from similar business / regulatory environments. Blumenritt and Nigh (2002) found that dependence within a network results in coordination in political effort. In summary, organizations (in this study nations—Kazakhstan and Russia) facing the same environmental dependencies are more likely to cooperate and use the same strategies (courses of reforms) in order to reduce environmental uncertainties.

When firms exhaust their ability to manage dependencies on the inter organizational level, Pfeffer and Salancik argue (p. 189), they inevitably start seeking assistance and protection of higher level players that could help them attain greater power. That is, through political actions, firms attempt to create an environment that is better for themselves and their interests. Empirical studies found support to this RDT proposition. Birnbaum (1985) examined various forms of business organizations—privately and publicly owned, for-

and non-for-profit entities—and found that as the dependence on regulatory agencies increases, firms are more likely to participate in political actions. This form of reduction in uncertainty, studies found, is more complex than other means of managing external dependence, which explains why firms actively seek outside directors who have connections with governments and other political structures. For example, Hillman et al. (1999) documented that firms whose managers are appointed to the US governmental agencies have higher abnormal returns. In emerging market settings, Peng and Luo (2000) documented improved market share for firms whose managers have strong political and social ties. In summary, the literature consistently found a link between the organizations' dependence on high level players and propensity to undertake a unilateral political action. This also suggests that at certain point, when other strategies to reduce external dependencies are exhausted, firms may abandon their cooperative mode and start acting more aggressively.

By the mid-1990s, it became clear that in order to achieve economic progress, CIS nations would have to start relying on external donors such as international organizations and foreign governments. That is, Kazakhstan and Russia exhausted their reliance on internal resources and had to seek help from the World Bank, IMF and others. The international agencies were quick to develop a course of reforms for the CIS countries and provide much needed monetary assistance. The radical economic reforms implemented in the CIS nations would not be possible without the assistance of these major external donors. Beginning in the 1990s, the CIS nations were also in stiff competition with each other to attract Foreign Direct Investments (FDIs). By 2003, there was a significant disparity in economic development between Kazakhstan and Russia, and the former's need for FDIs and hence, external resource dependence, was more significant compared to Russia. The two countries no longer operated in similar regulatory environments and experienced diverse financial needs. Russia became significantly more successful in restoring the national economy and securing internal resources for development of the capital markets system, compared to Kazakhstan. By 2003, Kazakhstan's reliance on external stakeholders—foreign donors—became more significant than interdependence with the Russian economy. The resource dependence theory, while recognizing the importance of both the internal and external contingencies (stakeholders), is silent about which form of dependence takes precedence over others in case multiple dependencies exist (Hillman et al. 2009). Nevertheless, the related *stakeholder theory* provides a constructive frame for identifying "primary" versus "secondary" stakeholders. Mitchell et al. (1997) suggest that this classification and stakeholder precedence should be formed based on the three attributes of power, legitimacy and urgency. By the early 2000s, all three attributes were greater in the case of external donors and hence, Kazakhstan's pressure from the external stakeholders was more significant than that from Russia.

Besides the technical assistance with a mass privatization program and investment support within the CIS, foreign donors such as the World Bank, IMF, USAID, etc. provided valuable advice regarding tax policy and administration, restructuring of Kazakhstan's treasury system, and public expenditure management (Timoshenko 2010, USAID 2015). More importantly, the IMF's technical assistance was a driving force behind Kazakhstan's transition from cash to accrual basis of accounting in 1990s, creating a new chart of accounts, and switching to internationally accepted reporting practices. The latter presumes converging national accounting standards with IFRS and adopting transparent reporting practices with enhanced investor protection norms. Adoption of the globally accepted high quality reporting practices is expected to attract foreign investor capital, which would stimulate development of the national economy. Indeed, as reported in prior studies, IFRS adoption is associated with increased FDIs and enhanced investor confidence (Amiram 2012, Chen et al. 2014). Additionally, studies examining the association between the level of investor protection and the IFRS adoption perspective found that less developed countries are more likely to adopt IFRS and surrender to international reporting standard setting organizations (Hope et al. 2006). This phenomenon can be best explained from the bonding perspective: by adopting IFRS countries effectively signal their commitment to transparent reporting and enhanced investor protection (see Coffee 1999, Stulz 1999).

As is evident from Table 6, Kazakhstan has heavily depended on the assistance of foreign organizations and nations, of which the IMF, the European Bank of Reconstruction and Development (EBRD), the Asian Development Bank, and the World Bank were the major donors. The total foreign aid as a fraction of GDP was 1.51 percent in the case of Kazakhstan, while it was only 0.68 percent in the case of Russia. Building on the institutional theory of DiMaggio and Powell (1983), that has many similar features with the RDT, and the notion of coercive isomorphism, Judge at el. (2010) reported that foreign aid is the major mechanism used by foreign agencies to bring about change in the national economy (p. 163). In support, the authors found that the extent of foreign aid is predictive of the degree of the IFRS adoption among 132 countries, including transitional economies. Consistent with this finding, Ashraf and Ghani (2005) and Hassan (2008) reported that the IMF was a major driving force behind a movement towards adoption of IFRS and other capital market reforms in Ghana and Egypt, respectively. Perera and Baydoun (2007) documented that one of the conditions accompanying the IMF's rescue package for Indonesia in 1997, following the Asian crisis, was revision of the national financial reporting legislation and adoption of international accounting standards. Accordingly, adoption of IFRS was inevitable for Kazakhstan due to its heavy reliance on foreign aid, which is supported by findings in the early study of Tyrrall et al. (2007).

It is worth mentioning that although the international donor organizations described herein provided invaluable monetary and technical assistance to emerging nations such as Kazakhstan, their interventions in the national course of reforms attracted much criticism. Arnold (2015) argues that these global market makers (World Bank, IMF, WTO, etc.) "Are not necessarily representative of broader societal interests," (p. 300) and that the World Bank and

IMF can be regarded as the colonizing influences arising from the process of globalization (see also Weetman 2006). Arnold (2005) noted that financial markets are often powerless in the face of inevitable changes driven by globalization. The analogy could be made with the global adoption of IFRS in that emerging markets are often under heavy influence of external sources to implement this reform. The influences of the major global donors on the reporting practices of emerging nations were identified in several studies. Mir and Rahaman (2005) analyzed the decision of Bangladeshi government to adopt IAS. The authors argue that this decision was made under pressure from international players such as IMF and that the nature of this reform was undemocratic, leading to high resistance and low compliance with IAS. Uddin and Tsamenyi (2005) examined the implications of the World Bank sponsored public sector reforms in Ghana. The authors concluded that, "Reporting to the monitoring agency did not make any positive changes to accountability and performance and was thereby unable to serve public interests". King et al. (2001) highlighted the challenges that the Romanian professional community faced in the late 1990s when the European-style reporting reforms were introduced.

In summary, it appears that adoption of IFRS in emerging markets was more of a legitimization step to raise credibility of arrangements between a country and international donors. As Weetman (2006) noted, "These influential institutions are imposing a cultural framework as well as institutional framework and that some aspects of this culture may be unfamiliar or even alien to the countries receiving aid" (p. 355).

Table 6. Foreign Aid and Foreign Direct Investment for Kazakhstan and Russia.

The Table reports the international donors' aid issued to Kazakhstan and Russia over the period of 1991–2012 (USD constant prices) and the relative Foreign Direct Investments (FDIs) in two periods: 1991–2005 and 2006–2014. Source: World Economic Outlook (2015), World Development Indicators (2015), USAID (2015).

Donor Commitment, USD, 1991–2012	Kazakhstan	Russia	Donor Total
Germany	538,599,731	27,306,924,266	27,845,523,997
World Bank - International Bank for Reconstruction and Development (IBRD)	6,589,750,110	19,418,780,327	26,008,530,437
European Bank for Reconstruction & Development (EBRD)	4,075,586,885	20,513,453,283	24,589,040,167
International Monetary Fund (IMF)	882,892,851	23,588,169,391	24,471,062,241
United States	1,310,532,347	9,934,360,142	11,244,892,489
Japan	1,137,861,652	2,456,735,783	3,594,597,435
World Bank - International Finance Corporation (IFC)	1,013,458,344	2,075,257,174	3,088,715,517
Asian Development Bank (ASDB)	2,929,263,167		2,929,263,167
European Communities (EC)	196,570,658	1,760,072,813	1,956,643,471
United Kingdom	44,679,732	756,191,407	800,871,139
Global Fund to Fight Aids, Tuberculosis and Malaria (GFATM)	76,147,844	369,282,233	445,430,077
Global Environment Facility (GEF)	75,227,684	298,277,324	373,505,008
France	95,770,397	242,179,146	337,949,544
Sweden	8,785,160	316,316,918	325,102,078
Canada	17,370,929	5,873,718	23,244,647
Portugal	11,841	256,503,390	256,515,231
Islamic Development Bank (ISDB)	203,966,673	8,215,373	212,182,046
World Bank - Carbon Finance Unit		154,746,949	154,746,949
Belgium	8,513,908	141,285,201	149,799,109
Spain	100,504,254	30,071,134	130,575,389
Switzerland	2,270,024	126,092,943	128,362,967
Finland	2,017,759	96,075,726	98,093,485
Norway	32,003,955	61,601,567	93,605,522
Netherlands	26,342,087	57,987,281	84,329,368
Austria	7,140,093	68,454,409	75,594,502

Table 6 cont'd

Korea	46,682,327		46,682,327
United Arab Emirates	44,974,456		44,974,456
Kuwait	34,347,262		34,347,262
United Nations Children's Fund (UNICEF)	17,047,724	3,685,414	20,733,138
Saudi Arabia	18,005,322		18,005,322
Italy	935,451	11,175,707	12,111,158
United Nations Development Programme (UNDP)	8,019,862	1,307,480	9,327,342
United Nations Population Fund (UNFPA)	7,048,829	2,088,245	9,137,074
Greece	3,216,482	5,873,718	9,090,200
Joint United Nations Programme on HIV/AIDS (UNAIDS)	3,673,203	4,203,278	7,876,481
OPEC Fund for International Development (OFID)	7,229,352		7,229,352
Czech Republic	3,151,840	1,314,444	4,466,283
OSCE	2,458,391		2,458,391
Denmark	2,055,533		2,055,533
Liechtenstein	93,038	1,918,590	2,011,628
United Nations Democracy Fund (UNDEF)	695,892	927,522	1,623,415
Luxembourg	931,797	8,513,908	9,445,705
Ireland	160,401	75,594,502	75,754,903
Australia	650,139	1,446	651,585
Lithuania		464,466	464,466
Estonia		1,446	1,446
New Zealand	145,748		145,748
Hungary	80,431	2,579	83,010
Monaco		79,086	79,086
Cyprus	58,740		58,740
Brazil	34,018		34,018
World Trade Organization (WTO)	32,541		32,541
Slovenia		26,241	26,241

Table 6 cont'd

Total Foreign Aid	19,576,996,861	110,160,085,970	129,737,082,831
Total GDP, billion USD, 1991–2012	1,292.4	16,156.7	
Total Foreign Aid as a fraction of GDP	1.51%	0.68%	

FDIs by period:

Foreign direct investment, annual net inflows (% of GDP), average for the 1991–2005 period	6.49%	1.09%
Foreign direct investment, annual net inflows (% of GDP), average for the 2006–2014 period	8.07%	3.15%

Next, the IFRS *implementation strategy* in case of Kazakhstan was rather unique, among all emerging nations. Kazakhstan was the first nation within the CIS region to require IFRS for banks (2004) and other public companies (2005), and this reform was implemented within a very short timeframe. This radical IFRS adoption strategy can be best explained from the RDT perspective, too. Pfeffer and Salancik (1978) suggested that the degree of the resource dependence defines the power and success of players in attracting external capital. Consequently, the pace of actions of the constituents (firms, nations) is defined by the availability of the external resources and the level of competition within a group. More recently, this resource dependence proposition has been adopted to explain the rationale behind a particular IFRS adoption strategy on a national level. For example, Alon and Dwyer (2014) examined 71 countries and reported that the higher the degree of resource dependency, the greater the likelihood that a country chooses to "require" IFRS adoption strategy, as opposed to the "not allow" or "permit" strategy. Accordingly, provided that Kazakhstan was in stiff competition for external resources and FDIs with other CIS nations, the fact that the country chose the "require" IFRS implementation strategy was justified.

Finally, the *timing* and particularly an early adoption of IFRS in Kazakhstan was considered a risky strategy by experts who argued that the country lacked necessary supporting infrastructure and hence, this reform was premature. Indeed, Tyrrall et al. (2007) reported that significant delays and technical issues were expected during the IFRS transition period and that *de facto* implementation of IFRS could be undermined due to insufficient resources and not so distant communist past of the country. As was noted previously, this decision to pioneer IFRS adoption was the strategic response of Kazakhstan to the capital market reforms and particularly, the IFRS adoption plan of its main competitor for FDIs—the Russian Federation. By the early 2000s, Kazakhstan and Russia had the most developed capital market systems, among all the CIS nations. Both countries established commitments to modernize the public accounting sector and in 2003, the Russia's Ministry of Finance issued a statement that beginning in 2004, Russian banks would switch to IFRS and that from 2005 all public companies would be required to prepared IFRS-based consolidated financial statements (Ministry of Finance of Russia 2015, IAS Plus Deloitte 2005). According to the resource dependence theory, this would indicate a shift of economic power and FDIs towards Russia and away from Kazakhstan. The resource dependence theory also predicts that mutually dependent actors, such as Russia and Kazakhstan whose economies are strongly interrelated, would adjust their actions according to changes in competition and power shifts. Indeed, in response to Russia's IFRS adoption plan, Kazakhstan's Ministry of Finance developed a similar plan within a short timeframe, indicating its commitment to require banks and other public companies to use IFRS on the same dates as Russia—in 2004 and 2005, respectively. Both countries, therefore, committed to implement this significant reform within the same deadlines.

Nevertheless, the next chain of events, first, disappointed foreign investors oriented towards the Russian economy and resulted in partial outflow of FDIs and, second, left investors in uncertainty regarding the progress of the implementation of the reporting reforms in Kazakhstan. Particularly, the Russian government first backed up from the announced plan to adopt IFRS for all public companies in 2005 (banks switched to IFRS in 2004) and later withdrew the plan in its entirety (until revisiting it in 2010). Kazakhstan, however, decided to proceed with the IFRS adoption initiative and closely followed the announced implementation pathway. Particularly, beginning in 2005, all listed companies must report in accordance with IFRS. One year later, they were joined by companies with significant public interest, which includes firms from extractive industries and those with significant governmental ownership (Ministry of Finance of Kazakhstan 2015). In addition, large companies with more than 250 employees or average annual incomes for the last three years of more than USD 20 million must also use IFRS for financial reporting purposes.

Table 6 reports details regarding the foreign aid received by Kazakhstan and Russia during the period of 1991–2012. The data strongly supports the previous propositions. In relative terms, Kazakhstan's foreign aid was around 1.51% of the total Gross Domestic Product (GDP) during this period, whereas for Russia the metric was only around 0.68%, therefore providing a strong evidence of Kazakhstan's higher external resource dependence, compared to Russia. Further, Kazakhstan's relative FDIs also exceeded those of Russia in the pre-reform 1991–2005 period, standing at 6.49% versus 1.09% of the GDP, respectively. Importantly, in the post-IFRS adoption period of 2006–2014 Kazakhstan's FDIs increased to 8.07% per year, on average. Russia's FDIs in this period, nevertheless, also increased to 3.15%, although Russia backed up from the IFRS adoption plan. These findings can be explained by the fact that the Russian government implemented other, non-IFRS related, capital market reforms aimed at improving the investment climate, including a merger of the two national stock exchanges and radical changes in the tax and legal legislature (see Kim 2013a, b).

In summary, until approximately 2003, Kazakhstan and Russia demonstrated cooperative strategies that manifested in parallelism of economic and capital market reforms. This is explained by the fact that the two countries initially operated in similar environments, experienced comparable financial needs, and faced the same uncertainties, following the collapse of the Soviet Union. At the same time, beginning in the mid-1990s, the two countries started accepting monetary aid from foreign donors such as the World Bank, the IMF, and others. By 2003, nevertheless, it became evident that Kazakhstan's internal resources were significantly more limited than those of Russia and that the country's dependence on external donors was more pronounced, compared to Russia. As a result of growing disparity in the economic development between the two countries, in 2005 Kazakhstan undertook the unilateral political action and announced mandatory adoption of IFRS for public companies, while Russia backed up from a similar plan. The evidence reported in Table 6 supports this and also shows that this risky strategy had a significant positive outcome, as Kazakhstan's net inflow of FDIs, in relative terms, was significantly higher than that of Russia post 2006. Moreover, Figure 2 demonstrates that KASE share price index significantly outperformed MICEX, the Russian stock market, share price index, and the sharp increase in the value of KASE index began in early 2006, shortly after Kazakhstan announced mandatory adoption of IFRS. From the middle of 2011, MICEX share price index outperformed KASE index due to capital market events such as formation of the Moscow Exchange and its successful public offering, accompanied by a series of regulatory reforms (Kim 2013a, b).

In the next chapter, I conduct a number of empirical tests that provide more direct evidence of benefits associated with adoption of IFRS in Kazakhstan.

Figure 2. Historical monthly correlation between KASE and MICEX share price indices: August 2000–April 2016.

Chapter 5. Empirical Analyses

In this chapter, I report the results of a series of empirical tests that provide important insight into the economic consequences of the IFRS adoption reform in Kazakhstan. I begin with analyzing the quality of reported information of Kazakhstani public firms in the post IFRS adoption period (chapter 5 1.) using the Ohlson (1995) price-earnings valuation model. The results of the empirical tests indicate that both earnings and book value per share are value relevant to investors following adoption of IFRS. Next, I compare the reporting quality of Kazakhstani and Russian public firms during the period of 2005–2011 (chapter 5.2). This is the period when the Kazakhstan's public firms were reporting under IFRS, whereas Russian firms used their local accounting standards to prepare annual reports. Comparing these two samples of public firms provides unique experimental settings due to the fact that Russia and Kazakhstan implemented capital market reforms in parallel, and consequently, the two countries' reporting environments were similar, with the major exception being that Kazakhstani public firms were required to use IFRS, unlike the Russian firms, during the period of 2005–2011. In 2012, Russia officially adopted IFRS, which is why the examined time period was limited by year 2011. Further, I examine the informational efficiency of the Kazakhstani stock market, using the KASE stock index daily returns (chapter 5.3). I document lack of weak-form efficiency and consequently, predictability of the Kazakhstani stock market. Therefore, investors are likely to be able to make systematic non-zero profits when trading with Kazakhstani stocks. Additionally, I do not find evidence of improvement in market efficiency over time and particularly, following adoption of IFRS. These findings are not surprising, however, provided that, first, the IFRS adoption reform was implemented contemporaneously with other capital market initiatives and it is therefore difficult to attribute the documented result to any one of them, and second, it can take several years for IFRS adoption benefits to materialize. Lastly, I document that following adoption of IFRS, several Kazakhstani blue chips applied for listing on one of the world's leading markets—London Stock Exchange—that gained popularity among emerging market firms over the past two decades due to introduction of Global Depositary Receipts programs that represent a convenient cross-listing mechanism (chapter 5.4). One of the major costs for firms associated with listing in London is due to the requirements to report in accordance with IFRS. Kazakhstani blue chips predominantly listed in London post 2005, following the national requirement to adopt IFRS, which is obviously due to reduced compliance costs, as they no longer had to prepare a second set of financials. I examine the market reaction to these firms' listing events and find that Cumulative Abnormal Returns increased for the majority of examined blue chips.

5.1. Value relevance of reported information in the post-adoption period

My initial intention was to examine changes in reporting quality of Kazakhstani public firms around the date of switch from the local reporting regime to IFRS, as was done in prior studies discussed above. Nevertheless, I found that the coverage of the KASE in Datastream is limited in early years and that the performance variables such as earnings and book value are reported beginning in 2001. Next, I attempted to hand-collect fundamentals and market data beginning in 1994 from firms' annual reports and the KASE records but found virtually no published financial statements and price data related to that early period. Hence, the direct examination of the changes in reporting quality in the pre- versus post-IFRS adoption period is impossible due to limited data in the pre-adoption period. In the additional tests, I examine changes in reporting quality over time, which can serve as an indirect assessment of the IFRS adoption consequences.

Prior studies extensively relied on the value relevance model of Ohlson (1995) to examine reporting quality of public firms in various international settings (see Alali and Foote 2012, Chen et al. 2001, Prather-Kinsey 2006, Kim 2013a, Kim 2016a, among others):

$$P_{it} = \beta_0 + \beta_1 EPS_{it} + \beta_2 BVPS_{it} + \varepsilon_{it}. \quad (1)$$

In model (1): P_{it}-share price of a firm *i* at year end *t*; EPS_{it}-reported earnings per share for a firm *i* for year *t*; $BVPS_{it}$-reported book value per share of a firm *i* as at the end of year *t*.

I identified 41 public companies (237 firm-year observations) that were listed on KASE and that had data on price, EPS and BVPS available in Datastream during the period of 2001–2014[13]. Table 7 presents the list of these public companies used in the empirical analysis. Table 8 reports the breakdown of the observations by year and provides the descriptive statistics for the main variables of the study for 237 firm-year observations. Panel A shows that the coverage of Kazakhstan's market was very limited prior to adoption of IFRS in 2004 (3 firm-year observations); there was a gradual improvement in the quantity of reported information, particularly beginning in 2009.

Interestingly, the examined public firms have significant extreme values, as is evident from Panel B. For example, the maximum value of EPS is 1,485, whereas the highest BVPS value is 1,126. The examined variables are characterized by a significant standard deviation and skewness. This evidence is consistent with findings in Kim's (2016a) study that examines Russian public firms that have similar backgrounds with Kazakhstani firms. Because of a significant number of extremely large values, model (1) estimation may suffer from the spurious scale effect problem: in large firms, price is naturally more correlated with a book value per share (Easton and Sommers 2003). This debate regarding the scale effects and its potential mitigation originated in the 1990s when the price model (1) based on Ohlson (1995) became prevalent. On one

---

13 Although the coverage of public firms generally improved in the most recent years, the availability of public information on individual companies' websites is very limited and is primarily in Russian rather than English. Therefore, Datastream appears to be the most complete source of financial information for Kazakhstani public firms.

hand, Barth and Clinch (2009) empirically demonstrated that a number of shares outstanding is an effective general proxy for scale (p. 281) and no further scaling in model (1) is required. Conversely, Easton and Sommers (2003) suggest that the *per share* estimation as in model (1) may not completely eliminate the scale effect. Hence, additional scaling in model (1) may be required.

Table 7. List of Kazakhstani public companies used in the empirical analyses: 41 public firms and 237 firm-year observations for which data on Price, EPS and BVPS were available in Datastream.

Company name / Year	2001	2002	2003	2004	2005	2006	2007	2008	2009	2010	2011	2012	2013	2014	Tot. firm-year
AKTOBE OIL EQU.PLANT									1	1	1	1	1	1	6
ASIA AVTO									1	1	1	1	1	1	6
ASIA SUGAR											1	1	1	1	4
ASTANAGAZSERVIS									1	1	1				3
ASTEL									1	1	1	1	1	1	6
ATFBANK									1	1	1	1	1	1	6
BANK CENTERCREDIT									1	1	1	1	1	1	6
BAYAN SULU											1	1	1	1	4
BTA BANK									1	1					2
CHIMPHARM									1	1	1				3
DANABANK									1	1	1	1	1	1	6
DELTA BANK									1	1	1	1	1	1	6
EKOTON									1	1	1	1		1	5
EURASIAN NATRES CORP.									1	1	1	1			4
FORTELEASING									1	1	1	1	1	1	6

Table 7 cont'd

HALYK KAZAKHINSTRAKH		1	1	6
HALYK SAVINGS BANK INSURANCE CO.LDN.ALMATY		1	1	6
JSC KAZMUNAIGAS		1	1	6
KANT DEAD		1	1	6
KAZAKHMYS		1	1	6
KAZAKHSTAN POTASH		1	1	4
KAZAKHTELCOM	1	1	1	7
KAZAKHTELCOM Frankfurt	1	1	1	10
KAZAKHTELCOM ADR 15:1	1	1	1	1	14
KAZAKHTELECOM PF		1	1	6
KAZINVESTBANK		1	1	6
KAZKOMMERTSBANK		1	1	6
KAZTRANSCOM		1	1	6
KAZTRANSOIL			1	2
KCEL			1	2
KMK MUNAI		1	1	6

Table 7 cont'd

MANGISTAU ELTY.DS.NET. MPANY						1	1	1	1	1	1	6
MANGISTAUMUNAIGAZ						1	1	1				3
MINERAL RES.OF CENTRAL ASIA						1	1		1	1		4
NURBANK						1	1	1	1	1	1	6
RAKHAT						1	1	1				3
REAL INVEST FINL.							1	1	1	1	1	5
RTS DECAUX						1	1	1	1	1	1	6
SAT & COMPANY						1		1	1	1		4
SENIM BANK						1	1	1	1	1	1	6
SHYMKENT MUNAI ONIMDERI						1	1	1	1	1	1	6
TEMIRBANK								1	1	1	1	4
UST KMGK.TTM.MGSUM.PLT.						1	1	1	1	1	1	6
Total	1	1	1	2	2	2	3	37	37	40	36	37	37	237

Next, there is no consensus in the literature regarding a choice of a scale variable to effectively mitigate the bias in model (1). Empirical studies, as a rule, provide little to no justification for the choice of a scale variable, which made me refer to the methodological literature where the scale effect mitigation techniques are discussed. Barth and Kallapur (1996) suggest that when scale effect exists and the true scale factor is known, then deflating model (1) by a scale factor should eliminate the coefficient bias. The authors examine several proxies for deflating (including sales, number of shares, book value, net income, share price) and report that these proxies only partially reduce bias. They suggest that including a scale factor (if it is known) as an additional explanatory variable would be preferred to scaling. Easton (1998), on the other hand, advocated for the deflating technique. He argues that when it comes to the choice of a deflator, "The predominant measure of scale is market capitalization" (p. 238), and that "price per share is the natural numeraire to be used to scale "per share" accounting data" (p. 238). Easton also suggests that deflating by other variables (e.g., sales or book value) changes the economic meaning of the dependent and independent variables (p. 242) that are affected by a variety of factors not implicit in the original Ohlson (1995) model. In a follow up study, Easton and Sommers (2003) demonstrate the validity of deflating the price model (1) by the market value (or price per share at year end) using the weighted least scares estimation technique (p. 26). The authors conclude that this technique is most effective in mitigating the scale bias in value relevance studies similar to the present study.

Finally, Barth and Clinch (2009) revisited the scale problem issue by examining a number of diagnostics tests and scale proxies (including lagged market value). They conclude that "no single estimation specification dominates the others for all types of scale effects and all inferences" (p. 255). The authors then suggested that the "price per share specification performs well in the presence of a variety of scale effects" (p. 281). Consistent with suggestions in Easton and Sommers (2003) and Barth and Clinch (2009), I estimate model (1) using the Weighted Least Squares (WLS) regression with the price per share at year end as a deflating factor (see also Kim 2016a). The results of this estimation are reported in Table 9. The coefficients on the EPS and BVPS variables are significantly positive (at one percent or better), suggesting that the information reported by Kazakhstani public firms is value relevant to investors. This is supportive of the IFRS adoption reform in Kazakhstan.

Next, as was noted previously, one of the limitations of this study is that I was unable to directly test for the changes in reporting quality of public firms prior to and after adoption of IFRS due to data limitations. Nevertheless, there were a number of significant improvements in the reporting environment in the post IFRS adoption period that were expected to make the reporting environment more transparent by attracting additional categories of firms to IFRS reporting. Particularly, in 2011 Kazakhstan's authorities announced the commitment to adopt IFRS for small and medium size companies (SMEs). This initiative was strongly supported by the World Bank and the IFRS Foundation which committed additional resources and provided trainings and workshops for interested parties in Kazakhstan to ensure a successful implementation of IFRS for SMEs. In the same year, these standards were translated into Russian and there was a detailed analysis of required changes in legislature performed by the World Bank. Small and medium size companies were allowed to elect to apply IFRS for SMEs.

Table 8. Descriptive Statistics.

The Table reports the distribution by year (Panel A) and the descriptive statistics for the 41 firms (237 firm-year observations) used in the empirical analyses (Panel B). Variables definitions: P = price per share; EPS = earnings per share; BVPS = book value per share; TA=total assets; MV = market value of equity (in millions); NoSh=number of shares of common stock outstanding (in thousands). All the variables were downloaded in USD.

Panel A. Distribution of 237 firm-year observations used in the empirical analyses by year.

Year	2001	2002	2003	2004	2005	2006	2007	2008	2009	2010	2011	2012	2013	2014	Total
No. Obs.	1	1	1	1	2	2	2	3	37	37	40	36	37	37	**237**

Panel B. Descriptive statistics for 237 firm-year observations used in the empirical analyses.

Variable	Firm-year obs.	Mean	Std. Dev.	Minimum	P25%	Median	P75%	Maximum
Price	237	85.46	211.73	0.01	4.1	8.76	61.07	1,190.54
EPS	237	35.16	155.92	-0.85	0.001	0.65	6.46	1,485.00
BVPS	237	42.86	119.05	-351.70	2.87	10.70	37.56	1,126.38
TA	237	2,426,948	4,525,244	5,801	58,069	163,235	2,227,530	23,195,142
MV	237	669	1,375	10	37	115	823	10,591
NoSh	237	830,954	3,997,492	92	1,500	10,526	161,077	43,595,810

Table 9. Empirical Analyses—value relevance of reported information post adoption of IFRS.

The Table reports the results from estimating model (1) for the sample of 41 firms (237 firm-year observations) over the period of 2001–2014. Variables definitions: P = price per share; EPS = earnings per share; BVPS = book value per share. The *, **, and *** indicate statistical significance at 10, 5 and 1 percent levels, respectively. The model estimated using the Weighted Least Square (WLS) approach and the price per share is used as the scaling factor.

$$P_{it} = \beta_0 + \beta_1 EPS_{it} + \beta_2 BVPS_{it} + \varepsilon_{it}.$$

Variable	No. Obs	Constant	EPS	BVPS	Adj R-squared
	237	0.02	0.01	0.04	0.10
t-stats		3.46***	2.62***	4.31***	

The discussed changes in the reporting environment raise an expectation of an improvement in reporting quality of public firms after 2011. Accordingly, I examine changes in value relevance of earnings and book value per share as a result of the mentioned improvements in the reporting environment by estimating the following modified Ohlson (1995) model:

$$P_{it} = \alpha_0 + \alpha_1 EPS_{it} + \alpha_2 BVPS_{it} + \alpha_3 Post + \alpha_4 EPS_{it}*Post + \alpha_5 BVPS_{it}*Post + \varsigma_{it}. \quad (2)$$

In model (2), all the variables are as previously defined and additionally, *Post* is a dummy variable equal to one for firm-year observations in the period of 2012–2014. The coefficients on the interaction terms *EPS*Post* and *BVPS*Post* are expected to be significantly positive if value relevance of information improved after 2011, following an additional course of improvements in the reporting environment. The results of this estimation are reported in Table 10. There is strong evidence that value relevance of information improved post 2011, and the coefficient on *BVPS*Post* is significantly positive (value=0.08***). There is no evidence of changes in relevance of EPS over time, however.

Table 10. Empirical Analyses—changes in value relevance of information post 2011.

The Table reports the results from estimating model (2) for the sample of 41 firms (237 firm-year observations) over the period of 2001–2014. Variables definitions: P = price per share; EPS = earnings per share; BVPS = book value per share; *Post* is a dummy variable equal to one for firm-year observations in the period of 2012–2014. The *, ** and *** indicate statistical significance at 10, 5 and 1 percent levels, respectively. The model estimated using the Weighted Least Square (WLS) approach and the price per share is used as the scaling factor.

$$P_{it} = \alpha_0 + \alpha_1 EPS_{it} + \alpha_2 BVPS_{it} + \alpha_3 Post + \alpha_4 EPS_{it} * Post + \alpha_5 BVPS_{it} * Post + \varsigma_{it}.$$

No. Obs	Constant	EPS	BVPS	Post	EPS* Post	BVPS* Post	Adj R-squared
237	0.015**	0.01**	0.03***	0.002	-0.005	0.08***	0.13

5.2. Comparison of value relevance of reported information for Kazakhstani and Russian public firms

As was noted in the previous chapter, one of the limitations of the empirical analyses regarding the IFRS adoption benefits for Kazakhstan's public firms is that the coverage of the Kazakhstan stock exchange is available predominantly in the post IFRS adoption period. Therefore, it is impossible to compare changes in reporting quality of public firms before and after the IFRS adoption event. Nevertheless, the unique CIS settings present a valuable opportunity to perform a comparative study of value relevance of information for Kazakhstani public firms that adopted IFRS compared to their Russian counterparts that did not. The official IFRS adoption date for the former group of companies was January 1, 2005, whereas for the latter IFRS was officially required in 2012. Therefore, it is possible to compare value relevance of reported information for the two groups of companies during the overlapping period of 2005–2011.

The main advantage of this setting is that Kazakhstan and Russia implemented their capital market reforms in parallel, as was discussed in the previous chapters, and the two countries share similar economic, legal, and historical backgrounds. The main limitation of such a comparative analysis is that the Russian market is significantly more mature and developed, compared to the Kazakhstani market (World Economic Forum 2016). The Russian market has a considerably more diverse investor base and a substantial portion of Russian blue chips have been cross-listed on the London Stock Exchange (LSE), which makes it more integrated with the global markets, compared to the Kazakhstani market. Thus, the Russian public firms' investors may have different informational needs, compared to Kazakhstani public firms, which would affect the value relevance of information for these two groups of companies.

I intend to estimate model (1) separately for Kazakhstani and Russian public firms over the period of 2005–2011, which significantly limits the sample of Kazakhstani public firms. To compare, in the previous section, the analyses were performed using 237 firm-year observations, while there are only 123 firm-year observations in the reduced 2005–2011 sample. Next, Kim (2016a) reported that prior to the official IFRS adoption year, 2012, the population of Russian public firms was not homogenous. Particularly, there was a significant number of Russian blue chips that cross-listed in the world's leading markets, primarily London, as Global Depositary Receipts (GDRs) beginning in the 1990s and were reporting in accordance with IFRS long before 2005. Furthermore, among non-blue chips, a significant portion of Russian public firms adopted IFRS voluntarily before they became mandatory in 2012. Consequently, for the comparative analyses, I need to exclude both blue chips and early voluntary IFRS adopters from the sample and should only focus on Russian public firms that continued using the Russian Accounting Standards (RAS) throughout the examined period of 2005–2011.

In Datastream I identified 848 firm-year observations related to the Russian public companies, RAS reporters, for which data on price, earnings, and book value per share were available for the examined period of 2005–2011. Therefore, the total sample that is used to implement the comparative analysis is 971 firm-year observations: 123 and 848 firm-year observations available for Kazakhstan and Russia, respectively.

Table 11 reports the results from estimating model (1) separately for Kazakhstani and Russian public firms. The coefficient on EPS is significantly positive, as expected, but only in the case of Kazakhstani public firms (value=1.17**), suggesting that earnings are value relevant to investors. The coefficient on BVPS is significant for both sample of firms at one percent or better (value=0.65*** and 0.81*** for Kazakhstan and Russia, respectively). Additionally, earnings have greater importance than book value based on the magnitude of the coefficient on EPS, compared to BVPS, for Kazakhstani public firms (value=1.17*** versus 0.65***). Overall, information appears to be of higher quality in the case of Kazakhstani firms reporting in accordance with IFRS.

Table 11. Comparative reporting quality for Kazakhstani versus Russian public firms.

The Table reports the results from estimating model (1) based on 123 and 848 firm-year observations related to Kazakhstani and Russian public firms, respectively over the period of 2005–2011. The latter group constitutes Russian companies that were not blue chips listed overseas and that did not adopt IFRS voluntarily prior to the official IFRS adoption year in Russia–2012. Variables definitions: P = price per share; EPS = earnings per share; BVPS = book value per share. The *, ** and *** indicate statistical significance at 10, 5 and 1 percent levels, respectively. The model estimated using the Weighted Least Square (WLS) approach and the price per share is used as the scaling factor.

$$P_{it} = \beta_0 + \beta_1 EPS_{it} + \beta_2 BVPS_{it} + \varepsilon_{it}.$$

	Kazakhstan				Russia			
Obs	Constant	EPS	BVPS	Adj R-sq	Obs	Constant	EPS	BVPS	Adj R-sq
123	17.22***	1.17*	0.65**	0.31	848	4.94**	0.32	0.81**	0.47

5.3. Examining changes in market efficiency over time, before and after IFRS adoption, using the KASE index

Prior literature examining the economic consequences of the IFRS adoption reform produced mixed findings, as was extensively discussed in the previous chapters. The main goal of these studies was to determine whether or not investors perceive the IFRS adoption reform beneficial to a country's economy. While most studies relied on value relevance price and returns based models, similar to the one employed in this study, to assess changes in reporting quality over time, some researchers argue that examination of the IFRS adoption consequences on a national level should start with more basic tests, such as the market efficiency (Alnodel 2015). The main expectation of the market participants is that following adoption of IFRS, the stock market becomes more efficient. There is a significant amount of empirical evidence regarding emerging markets efficiency, and most studies report that they are informationally inefficient. To my knowledge, there is no empirical evidence regarding the efficiency of Kazakhstan's stock market, which motivates this empirical investigation.

Extant literature primarily examined the weak-form efficiency of a stock market (Fama 1965). The efficient market hypothesis (EMH) in this case suggests that past prices of a stock are reflected in today's stock price and hence, technical analysis cannot be used to predict and outperform the market. This form of market efficiency implies that stock returns follow a random walk pattern and hence, are unpredictable. The weak-form of the market efficiency was extensively investigated in various settings and using different techniques.

In an early study, Hall and Urga (2002) reported that the Russian stock market was informationally inefficient. The most recent study of Kim (2016b) concurs with these findings: first, information is asymmetrically reflected in price series of Russian cross-listed firms and second, Russian stocks' return series are predictable. Therefore, investors are likely to make systematic profits on trading with Russian stocks. In contrast, Abrosimova et al. (2005) documented some evidence in favor of a weak-form efficiency, using monthly data. Similarly, Ansotegui et al. (2009) found that the market is efficient with respect to pricing Egyptian stocks. When examining the market efficiency for the BRIC countries, Chong et al. (2012) concluded that these markets are informationally inefficient, and the Russian market is the least efficient of all. Similarly, Thiele (2014) rejected the market efficiency hypothesis for the Chinese equity returns. Contrary to this evidence, Alam et al. (1999) documented that return indices of Bangladesh, Hong Kong, Malaysia and Taiwan, indeed, followed a random walk and therefore, were weak-form efficient. Overall, prior literature produced conflicting evidence regarding the informational efficiency of emerging markets.

I test the weak-form efficiency of Kazakhstan's market in the following way. First, I downloaded daily closing values of the main index of the Kazakhstan Stock exchange—KASE—beginning December 7, 2000 when the value of this index was set to 100 (base value) until April 27, 2016 (KASE archive, 2016). This sample includes 4,050 daily observations. Next, I computed the daily returns, following the methodology adopted in prior literature:

$$R_t = Ln(KASE_t / KASE_{t-1}). \quad (3)$$

In the above model, R_t is the market return on day t, $KASE_t$ and $KASE_{t-1}$ are the value of the KASE price index at the end of day t and $t-1$, respectively. Next, I used a variety of techniques to examine the weak form of Kazakhstan's market efficiency using computed KASE returns. Those are discussed next.

5.2.1. Autocorrelation Test

Prior studies extensively relied on the autocorrelation test that is aimed at determining repeating patterns in observations for the same variable over time (Alnodel 2015). If the serial correlation of return observations is zero, then they follow a random walk, therefore supporting the weak form of the efficient market hypothesis. On the contrary, presence of serial correlation indicates that observations are not independent and do not follow a random walk pattern, thus rejecting the EMH. Under this test, the null hypothesis is that the value of autocorrelation coefficients is not significantly different from zero.

Table 12 reports the result of the serial correlation test for 4,049 daily return observations for KASE, computed in accordance with model (3). For all 20 lags, the values of Q-stat are significantly different from zero and therefore, the null hypothesis of no serial correlation in return observations is rejected at one percent or better. The results remain the same if the analysis is extended beyond 20 lags. This evidence rejects the weak form efficiency of Kazakhstan's market.

5.2.2. The unit root test

Prior literature also relied on the unit root test to examine the market efficiency (Alnodel 2015, Kim 2016b). Series that follow a random walk pattern, which is consistent with a weak form market efficiency, have a unit root I(1) and are non-stationary. On the contrary, series are stationary if their first- and second-order moments are time-invariant. Such series have a tendency to mean-revert and are also referred to as series with no unit root, or 'series I(0)'. I test KASE return series for stationarity applying the Augmented Dickey-Fuller (ADF) test with Mac-Kinnon (1996) one-sided p-values. The results of this test are reported in Table 13. The statistic value of -82.9*** (significant at one percent or better) is significantly smaller than the Mac-Kinnon (1996) critical values, therefore rejecting the null hypothesis of non-stationarity in KASE returns. The implication of this is that in case of a structural break caused by a shock, the stock prices quickly return to the same path as before the shock. Stationarity in return series is indicative of predictability, implying that Kazakhstan's stock market is inefficient. For robustness, I implemented the unit root test allowing for a possibility of a breakpoint in the data. The unreported results are consistent with those reported in Table 13, rejecting the market efficiency hypothesis. Lastly, I partitioned the examined sample into pre IFRS period (December 2000–December 2005) and post-IFRS period (January 2006–April 2016) and performed the unit root test separately for these two sub periods. The results of this test suggest that the return series are predictable in both sub periods. Therefore, in the post IFRS adoption period there was no improvement in informational efficiency of Kazakhstan's stock market. This, however, is only indirect evidence regarding the benefits or costs of IFRS adoption. First, IFRS adoption is a lengthy process, and it can takes several years before benefits of this important reform fully materialize. Second, although being an important event, IFRS adoption was only one initiative in the pool of capital market initiatives launched by the Kazakhstani government throughout the examined period. Therefore, it is difficult to disentangle the impact of IFRS adoption from the impact of other concurrent changes in regulations on the information environment and attribute the documented result to any one of them.

To conclude, the evidence reported in this section strongly rejects the weak form efficiency of Kazakhstan's stock market. This is not surprising, however, given the relative immaturity of Kazakhstan's capital market system. This evidence is also in line with the inefficiency of the Russian market reported in Kim (2016b) that has many similarities with Kazakhstan's market, but is significantly more established.

Table 12. Serial correlation test for KASE daily returns. Examined period: December 2000-April 2016.

Autocorrelation lag	AC	PAC	Q-Stat	Prob
1	-0.259	-0.259	271.55	0.000
2	0.055	-0.013	283.63	0.000
3	0.010	0.023	284.07	0.000
4	0.034	0.046	288.75	0.000
5	0.010	0.031	289.15	0.000
6	-0.002	0.006	289.17	0.000
7	0.003	0.001	289.21	0.000
8	0.044	0.046	297.19	0.000
9	-0.033	-0.012	301.56	0.000
10	0.011	-0.004	302.04	0.000
11	0.018	0.020	303.42	0.000
12	-0.009	-0.001	303.71	0.000
13	0.034	0.032	308.31	0.000
14	0.011	0.030	308.81	0.000
15	0.032	0.042	313.00	0.000
16	0.011	0.027	313.47	0.000
17	-0.007	-0.001	313.67	0.000
18	0.019	0.010	315.12	0.000
19	0.016	0.019	316.12	0.000
20	-0.031	-0.026	319.93	0.000

Source: www.kase.kz/archive.

Table 13. Properties of KASE returns series. Examined period: December 2000–April 2016.

		t-Statistic	Prob.*
Augmented Dickey-Fuller test statistic		-82.90042	0.0001
Test critical values:	1% level	-3.431781	
	5% level	-2.862057	
	10% level	-2.567089	

*MacKinnon (1996) one-sided p-values.

The KSE returns series are tested for being stationary and the null hypothesis is that series have a unit root (nonstationary), against the alternative hypothesis that series are stationary. The Augmented Dickey-Fuller test is performed and the results of the test are assessed against the Mac-Kinnon (1996) critical values. The number of lags is determined based on the Schwarz criteria and the results of the test strongly reject the null hypothesis at 1 percent or better, indicating that returns series are stationary.

5.4. Kazakhstani blue chips cross-listed in London: The market reaction to the cross-listing event

As was noted in the previous chapters, beginning in 2005 IFRS became required for all public companies in Kazakhstan. The results of the empirical tests reported above indicate that overall, IFRS adoption was beneficial for Kazakhstani public firms. First, reported earnings and book value of equity are value relevant for investors and second, investors perceive earnings of Kazakhstani public firms to be value relevant, compared to earnings of their Russian counterparts that continued reporting under the local accounting standards.

The IFRS adoption, nevertheless, is considered a global event in that the benefits of IFRS adoption are expected to extend beyond the borders of individual nations choosing to adopt them. A relatively new stream of research that examines the economic consequences of IFRS adoption takes on a novel perspective and relies on the economic theory of networks to explain nations' decisions to adopt IFRS. Particularly, Ramanna and Sletten (2016) demonstrate that as more jurisdictions with economic ties to a given country adopt IFRS, perceived benefits from lowering transactions costs to foreign users of reported information increase. Foreign users who are familiar with IFRS experience lower informational barriers when analyzing foreign companies' financial reports, which will lead to higher valuation benefits for foreign companies using IFRS and eventually, for the nations they represent. Furthermore, the authors find the relatively smaller countries (such as Kazakhstan) have differentially higher responses to the net benefits of IFRS adoption. This is only true, however, when foreign investors have access to local companies' stocks. The reporting regulation in Kazakhstan, especially in the early years of the formation of the national capital market system, provided very limited opportunities for foreign investors' participation in the equity stock transactions, which was similar to the case of Russia (Kim 2013a, b).

Nevertheless, an alternative route that local companies can pursue to gain access to foreign investors and increase their visibility is to cross-list their shares on an overseas market that has a deep investor base. Studies of Kim (2013a, b) provide extensive evidence of the benefits associated with this visibility strategy for Russian blue chips. She finds that in the long-term, Russian blue chips cross-listed in London as GDRs significantly outperform both the local and the native UK market stocks, and their Cumulative Abnormal Returns over a three-year period reach 60 percent. Most importantly, in recent years, the Russian blue chips have led the Global Depositary Receipts sector of the LSE by a significant margin, compared to firms from other markets. Overall, this global recognition strategy pioneered by the Russian blue chips had a significant positive outcome for both the companies listed as GDRs and the Russian market as a whole, which is consistent with the evidence in Ramanna and Sletten (2016).

The Main Market of the London Stock Exchange has become the primary cross-listing destination for firms from emerging markets, beginning in 1994 when the first sponsored GDR program was registered. One of the factors explaining the overwhelming popularity of this market, compared to other global markets such as the New York Stock exchange and Nasdaq of the US, is the lower reporting and corporate governance obligations with which GDR listed firms must comply prior to and following a listing event. This lower reporting cost for GDRs, compared to more rigorous obligations for American Depositary Receipts (ADRs), was the major driver behind, first, migration of foreign firms to London from the US markets following the costly Sarbanes-Oxley regulation, and second, increased popularity in the GDR instruments among emerging market firms. The net benefits of this "light touch" reporting approach advocated for by the UK regulators were uncertain, however, and GDRs were subject to much criticism from various market participant groups. The challengers of this simplified regulations approach suggested that benefits of cross-listing as GDRs would not materialize and that eventually there will be decline in the number of these programs. The statistics, however, show otherwise and not only the number of GDRs was increasing over time but also the most successful Initial Public Offering (IPO) events in history were completed via London-based GDR programs (e.g., Gazprom and VTB of Russia).

Table 14 provides important insight into the extent of the reduced reporting obligations and corporate governance compliance requirements for GDRs compared to the competing cross-listing instruments—ADRs—that originated in the 1920s and from which GDRs have taken a considerable market share over the past two decades. GDRs are not required to report quarterly, release less information to the market participants, and are officially exempt from compliance with the UK's Corporate Governance Code, although some GDRs voluntarily adhere to this regulation. Exchange-listed GDRs, however, have to fully comply with IFRS and provide a detailed history of accounts prior to cross-listing. Their financial statements must be audited in accordance with International Standards on Auditing (ISA) and as a rule, these firms are audited by one of the Big Four companies, namely Deloitte, Ernst & Young, KPMG, and PricewaterhouseCoopers.

Table 14. Comparative reporting obligations for exchange-listed ADRs and GDRs.

Type	Pre-listing requirements	US Securities Acts / EU Directive	Listing Alternatives	Submitted forms with SEC / FSA	Reporting frequency	Accounting reconciliation requirements	SOX or equivalent
Level II ADR	Three-year audited financial statements; working capital statement; pro-forma statements due	1933, 1934	NYSE, NASDAQ, Amex	F-6, 20-F*, F-6K	Quarterly (reviewed) and annual (audited)	Reconciliation of the major Balance Sheet and Income Statement items to the US GAAP*	Full compliance with SOX provisions
Level III ADR (capital raising)	to change in business	1933, 1934	NYSE, NASDAQ, Amex	F-1, F-6, F-6K, 20-F*	Quarterly (reviewed) and annual (audited)	Full reconciliation of financial statements to the US GAAP*	Full compliance with SOX provisions
Level II & Level III GDRs (capital raising)	12–18 months pre-listing history of accounts, no working capital statement or change in business pro-forma required**	EU Prospectus Directive, FSA Chapter 18 and provisions of Rule 144A if combined with US private offering	London Stock Exchange Main Market combined with offering on US PORTAL	None/Annual report	Interim (unaudited), annual (audited)	Reconciliation of the major Balance Sheet and Income Statement items to the IAS (prior to 2001) and IFRS (after 2001)	No equivalent of SOX; no requirement to comply with the Combined Code on Corporate Governance

Source: Bank of New York Mellon; Citibank; London Stock Exchange (website and archives); Financial Services Authority (FSA). * In January 2008 the SEC adopted an amendment to the Form 20-F. In particular, it eliminated the requirement to reconcile financial statements to the US GAAP for foreign private issuers reporting in accordance with IFRS as issued by the IASB. The amendment applies to financial statements with financial year ending post November 15, 2007 (SEC—Federal Register - Release Nos. 33–8879; 34–57026; International Series Release No. 1306; File No. S7-13-07). ** Despite the fact that these statements are not required, some GDR-listed companies have chosen to voluntarily increase the scope of reported information and disclosure in order to satisfy investor information needs and signal their commitment to transparent reporting.

The study of Kim and Pinnuck (2014) was among the first works to provide direct empirical evidence of the benefits associated with cross-listed GDRs on the Main Market of the LSE. The authors documented significant decline in the cost of capital for GDRs as a result of cross-listing and more importantly, the magnitude of decline in the cost of capital for GDRs was comparable to that for ADRs that are subject to greater scrutiny. The authors explain this finding by the fact that the two channels through which information asymmetry is decreased after cross-listing—public disclosure and analysts—are substitutive and make equally important contributions to information risk reduction, therefore leading to similar cost of capital decline for ADRs and GDRs.

The previous discussion suggests that, first, Kazakhstani firms could increase their visibility and get access to external investors by listing as GDRs, which proved to be successful for their Russian counterparts, and second, significant valuations benefits should accrue to firms pursuing this route. One of the major costs associated with GDR listing is compliance with IFRS, as is evident from Table 14. As such, it is unlikely that Kazakhstani companies would pursue a GDR listing route prior to the official adoption date in 2005. Beginning in 2006, however, the total cost of GDR listing should be lower due to full compliance with IFRS, making a GDR listing route more attractive for them. The statistics from Datastream confirms this proposition. Only one Kazakhstani company—Kazkommertsbank—cross-listed as a GDR prior to 2005 (in 1998). There were 4 blue chip companies that pursued a GDR listing after 2005: Kazmunajgas (October 10 2016, *Oil and Gas*), Halyk Bank (December 2006, *Banks*), Kazakhstan Kagazy (July 2007, *Paper packaging and recycling*), and Alliance Bank (July 2007, *Banks*).

What remains uncertain, nevertheless, is whether or not foreign investors perceived the information released by these companies credible. If the IFRS-based reports, indeed, were viewed as reliable sources of financial information than one would expect investors to exhibit a positive market reaction to a cross-listing event. Conversely, the market reaction to a cross-listing event would be negative if investors express lack of credibility towards the IFRS-based public information released by Kazakhstani blue chips.

Accordingly, I examine the market reaction to a GDR listing event for the 4 mentioned Kazakhstani blue chips. I use a 100-day window surrounding a cross-listing event and examine the behavior of Cumulative Abnormal Returns (CARs) that prior literature used as a proxy for firm value (Ritter 1991, Kim 2013b). I follow the methodology in the seminal study of Ritter (1991) that examined the post-listing performance of firms raising capital through an IPO. The market-adjusted (abnormal) return ar_{it} for firm i on day t is:

$$ar_{it} = r_{it} - Rm_t. \quad (4)$$

The average market-adjusted return for the sample of n stocks on a day t is defined as:

$$AR_t = \frac{1}{n}\sum_{i=1}^{n} ar_{it}. \quad (5)$$

The cumulative abnormal returns for a period from day x to day y is then:

$$CAR_{x->y} = \sum_{t=x}^{y} AR_t \quad (6)$$

First, I used the FTSE All—Share index that covers constituents with the combined value of approximately 98 percent of the total UK market capitalization. This UK market monthly return index (Rm_t) was selected as a benchmark for CARs due to the fact that all examined Kazakhstani blue chips have a GDR tranche listed on the Main Market of the LSE. Second, I rely on the local market KASE price index to compute CARs.

Figure 3 depicts the behavior of CARs from day 0 (cross-listing day) until day 100 following a GDR cross-listing event for Kazmunajgas. Over the examined window, CARs experience an overall increase and reached 23.48 percent and 1.65 percent on day 100 based on the FTSE All share index and KASE index, respectively. Therefore, it appears that Kazmunajgas outperformed both the local and the UK firms, although the KASE-based increase in CARs is significantly lower than that based on the FTSE All—Share index. This evidence suggests that investors reacted positively to the firm's GDR cross-listing event.

Figure 4 provides details on the behavior of CARs following a GDR cross-listing event for Halyk Bank. Although the average daily CARs for this firm were 14 percent and 3.9 percent based on the FTSE All share and KASE price indices, respectively, by the end of the examined 100-day window the CARs were only 2.6 percent and -3.83 percent. Therefore, in the case of Halyk Bank, the conclusion about the investors' reaction to the GDR listing event depends on the choice of the benchmark: unambiguously, there was a positive reaction to the GDR listing event based on the UK price index, whereas the local market KASE index produced a mixed picture.

Figure 5 portrays changes in firm value for Kazakhstan Kagazy. It is evident that this company's positive changes in CARs were more pronounced, compared to the previous two companies. The average daily CARs over the examined 101-day window were 12 percent and 18 percent based on the FTSE All share and KASE price indices, respectively, while on day 100, these values reached 22.5 percent and 31.2 percent. Therefore, Kazakhstan Kagazy outperformed both the local and the UK market firms in the post-listing period. Interestingly, despite an impressive performance, this company eventually delisted from the LSE in March of 2016, as a result of the litigation brought by the Kazakhstan Kagazy Group against its former shareholders and directors who were presumably involved in financial fraud. At present, the case is being heard in the High Court of London.

Lastly, Figure 6 reports the post-listing changes in CARs for Alliance Bank. The picture is strikingly different from the previously discussed results for Kazmunajgas, Halyk Bank and Kazakhstan Kagazy. Clearly, this company significantly underperformed based on both the UK and the local KASE price indices. On day 100, CARs were -66.7 percent and -57.8 percent based on the two benchmarks. It appears that throughout the period of 2005-2008, the Bank's Chairman and his brother implemented a fraudulent financing scheme that involved several off-shore companies. In 2008, the Bank started having liquidity problems and in 2009, it was on the verge of collapse. In 2011, the company brought the case against the former Chairman to London's High court that put a block on his assets. Kazakhstan's national court issued a ruling that the financing scheme implemented by the Chairman violated the local legislature. The Bank's GDR program in London was suspended in 2009 and the company has been trying to recover the massive losses as a result of the off balance sheet transactions, estimated to cause damage in the amount of 1.1 billion USD. Interestingly, the shareholders of Alliance Bank decided to proceed with the GDR listing plans in 2007, despite the fact that the Bank was already amidst the liquidity crises, of which foreign investors were aware, as is evident from the significant underperformance and sharp decline in market value of the company in the post-listing period.

In summary, three of the four examined Kazakhstani blue chips that listed in London following the IFRS adoption reform in Kazakhstan experienced positive changes in firm value following a GDR listing event, suggesting that their IFRS-based financial statements provided reliable information and were perceived credible by foreign investors. Nevertheless, these findings are only indirect evidence in favour of benefits of adoption of IFRS, as listing on the high quality market such as the LSE entails other obligations, besides full IFRS compliance, such as disclosing a variety of supplemental information (history of accounts, management forecasts, working capital statements, etc.). Additionally, investors expect GDR-listed firms to adhere to stringent corporate governance norms.

Prior literature produced mixed findings regarding the post-listing performance of cross-listed firms (see Foerster and Karolyi 1999, Miller 1999). The study of Kim (2013b) that is most relevant to this work examined the short- and long-term post-listing performance for Russian and CIS blue chips (including several GDRs from Kazakhstan) that are either single- or dual-listed as GDRs in London. The author found that both categories of firms significantly underperformed compared to the UK firms in the short-run. However, over a three-year period, there was a significant positive change in CARs that reached 40 percent and 60 percent by the end of year three in the case of single- and dual-listed GDRs.

Interestingly, Kim (2013b) documented that the Russian and CIS firms are predominantly single-LSE listed or reverse cross-listed. The latter strategy suggests that a firm first lists on a foreign market and subsequently becomes listed domestically. The evidence in Kim and Pinnuck (2014) suggests that emerging market firms often choose these strategies, unlike their peers from developed markets that prefer a "conventional" cross-listing mechanism of being listed on a local market first and subsequently cross-listing on a foreign exchange. The examined blue chips fall into the same pattern as other emerging markets' firms. Particularly, Kazmunajgas was single-listed on the LSE, whereas Halyk Bank, Kazakhstan Kagazy and Alliance Bank were reverse cross-listed, and for them the GDR listing in London was the first listing. As discussed in Kim (2013b), the strategy of foregoing the local market and selecting a foreign platform as the main listing destination is very risky. Nevertheless, it appears that it has positive outcomes in that three of the examined blue chips were subject to enhanced valuation benefits following a GDR listing event, as was noted previously.

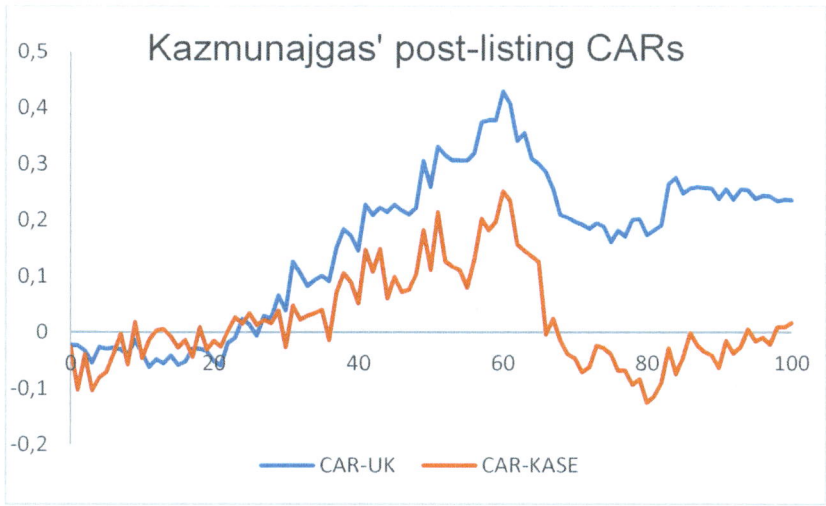

Figure 3. Kazmunajgas' post-listing CARs.

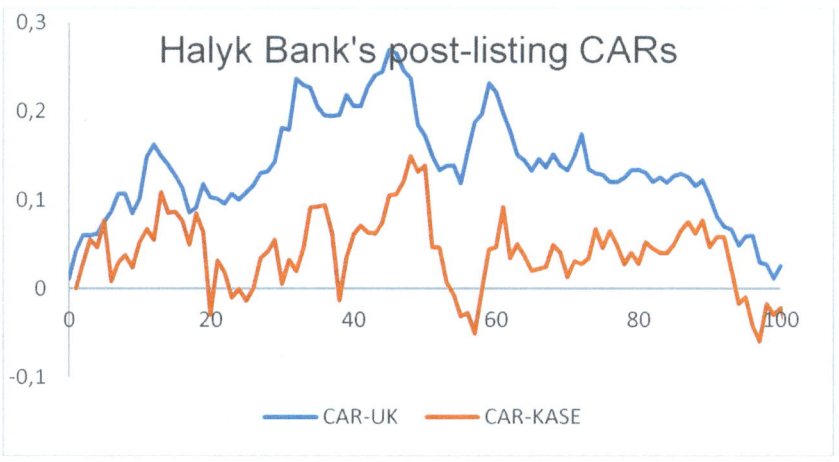

Figure 4. Halyk Bank's post-listing CARs.

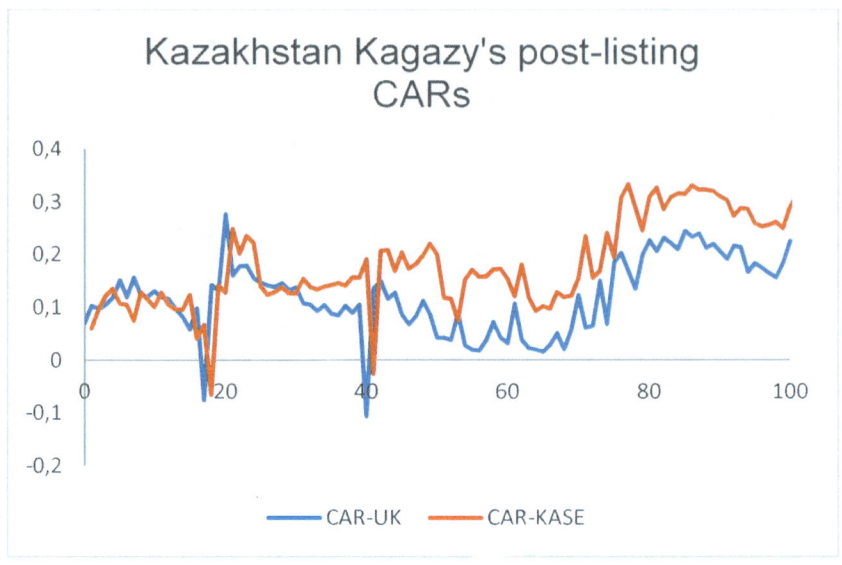

Figure 5. Kazakhstan Kagazy's post-listing CARs.

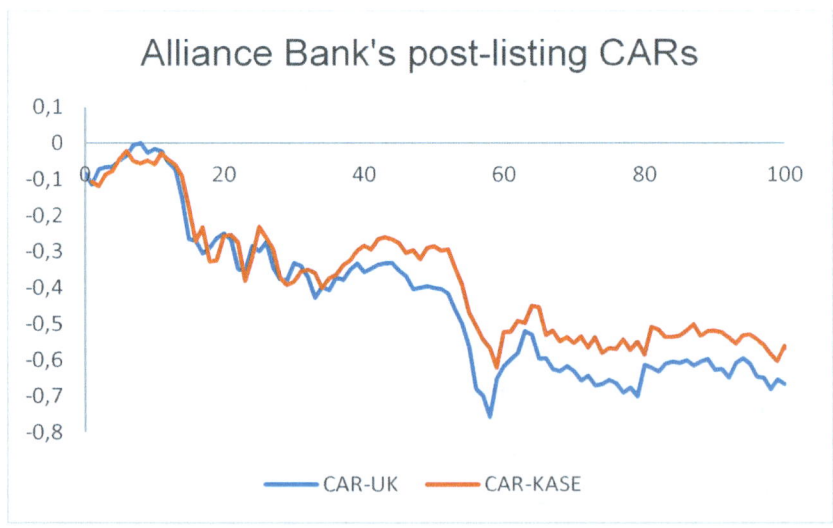

Figure 6. Alliance Bank's post-listing CARs.

Summary of the results of the empirical tests reported in this manuscript

First, it appears that earnings and book value of equity are value relevant to investors in the post IFRS adoption period. Due to limitations of the data collection process and poor coverage of Kazakhstan's stock market in databases, I was unable to perform pre-post analyses of changes in the reporting quality of public firms. Second, Kazakhstani public firms reported higher quality information, compared to their Russian peers, during the period of 2005–2011 when the former companies adopted IFRS, while the latter were exempt from the IFRS reporting requirement. Next, there was an increase in value relevance of information post 2011, following introduction of IFRS for SMEs and medium sized businesses. Further, it appears that market participants reacted positively to a London GDR listing event of Kazakhstani blue chips (except for one case) that reported in accordance with IFRS. On the other hand, there is no evidence of improvement in informational efficiency of Kazakhstan's stock market post adoption of IFRS. This suggests that this initiative was only one reform in the pool of capital market developments required to improve the efficiency of Kazakhstani market.

Chapter 6. Future perspectives.

6.1. Kazakhstan's success and future perspectives

On October 1, 1997 the president of Kazakhstan, Nursultan Nazarbayev, declared a strategic development plan for the nation, named "Kazakhstan 2030". The initiative calls for creating the competitive open market economy that would turn Kazakhstan into one of the leading emerging nations by the year 2030. The strategy also emphasizes the importance of foreign investments to the national economy and the perspective for integration of Kazakhstan into the global market system. The new economic model is based on the promotion of the private sector, free competition, and development of the national stock market system (Nazarbayev 1997). In 2006, president Nazarbayev initiated the "Strategy of Kazakhstan's joining 50 most competitive countries in the world" that developed additional steps toward achieving the goal of Kazakhstan's entering the pool of the most competitive nations globally (Ayagan et al. 2011). In 2012, the president of Kazakhstan issued an even more ambitious plan, "Kazakhstan 2050", that calls for further strengthening of the nation's global positions and is aimed at making Kazakhstan one of the top 30 nations by the year 2050. In this plan, the president prioritizes international cooperation with other nations and enhanced economic and trading diplomacy with multiple external stakeholders, such as foreign investors (Kazakhstan 2050, 2012).

At present, almost two decades after the first of the noted strategic initiatives was launched, it is possible to assess the preliminary outcomes of their implementation. During the period of 1997–2011, the volume of the national economy grew from 1.7 to 28 trillion Tenge, and the average annual GDP growth rate was 7.6 percent, which is higher than in other CIS countries (Ayagan et al. 2014). Among the CIS nations, Kazakhstan is ranked second, after Russia, in the production of oil and natural gas condensate. The volumes of exports of these minerals have been growing at a fast pace. Additionally, Kazakhstan was among the largest producers and exporters of refined copper and also possesses one of the largest gold deposits in the world (Ayagan et al. 2011). By some estimates, the economic growth in Kazakhstan was higher than anticipated, leading to substantial inflow of foreign investments in the national economy. Collectively, these indicators suggest that Kazakhstan's implementation of the "2030" strategy has had a notable success and that the country's future perspectives are optimistic.

From the inception of the national economic reforms, it was obvious that the progress would not occur without injections of foreign capital, as was extensively discussed in the previous chapters. In 1997, the government introduced the law "On state support of Direct Investments" that provided tax exemptions and guaranteed other concessions for projects implemented with foreign capital (Ayagan et al. 2011). As a result, by the end of the 1990s, foreign stakeholders committed about 60 billion USD in long-term investments to Kazakhstan. In 1997, the GDP per capita in Kazakhstan was 165 USD of FDIs, which was five times higher than in Russia, and there has been positive growth in this metric over the years (World Bank 2015). As reported in Ayagan et al. (2011), by 2007, not only had Kazakhstan occupied first place in terms of the per capita attracted investments within the CIS, but it was also second only to Hungary in the former Soviet Union bloc.

Such a success in national economic development can be attributed to Kazakhstan's enormous supplies of fossil fuels and minerals that attract foreign investors, but without doubts, it is also due to the radical changes in the national stock market system, of which adoption of international reporting standards is a critical component. Investors are unlikely to commit significant resources to companies whose reporting practices are not transparent and are of poor quality. In support of this conjecture, in the previous chapters there was a strong correlation reported between the growth in volume of FDIs and the reforms in the capital market system.

In summary, since declaring independence, Kazakhstan has achieved remarkable growth in the national economy and created an impressive capital market system that is recognized globally and to which foreign investors commit considerable resources. At present, the country is known as one of the most successful CIS nations and Kazakhstan, without doubts, is considered an important global player rather than simply a local force.

6.2. The future of the IFRS reporting practices in Kazakhstan

In the previous chapter, I reported empirical evidence suggesting that overall, the IFRS adoption reform was beneficial for Kazakhstani public firms and the stock market as a whole. This does not mean, however, that implementation of IFRS went smoothly and that the professional community fully complied with the Western-style reporting practices.

Djakisheva (2014) discussed the progress of the IFRS adoption reform in the first years of its implementation. The author outlined the major obstacles that slowed down the pace of this reform, many of which were anticipated when Kazakhstan officially announced mandatory adoption of IFRS. First, the translation of the official version of IFRS (as issued by the IASB) into Russian and native Kazakh is incomplete and inaccurate, and multiple corrections are not communicated to professional accountants on a timely basis. Second, similar to the IFRS implementation problems identified in the case of Russia (IAS Plus 2016), the "substance over form" concept that applies to various types of revenue/expense transactions under IFRS has very limited implication in Kazakhstan. Conformity to tax rules that require recognition of transactions based on the documents received, and thus the legal form of a transaction, prevails. Next, Djakisheva (2014) points out that application of the fair value concept that IFRS requires or allows for some types of assets and liabilities is limited due to the reluctance of financial statements preparers to apply judgement and search for market information. Tax authorities commonly oppose application of the fair value concept and implementation of impairment tests in the tax-based reports. In addition, information about related parties and associated companies is often unavailable, which limits the transparency of the disclosed information and contradicts the IFRS requirements to disclose the nature of such transactions.

Overall, it appears that the Kazakhstani professional society has faced similar challenges upon implementation of IFRS as other CIS countries (Russia) and emerging markets. In their earlier study, Tyrrall et al. (2007) envisioned some of the obstacles identified here and noted that culture, mentality, and lack of guidance would make the IFRS adoption process very problematic and slow. Djakisheva (2014) also points out to the inconsistency between the IFRS reporting rules and local legislature. For example, the national legislature requires the asset to be fully transferred into the ownership of the lessee at the end of the useful life of the finance lease contract, whereas under IFRS this is not a major condition for classification of the contract as a finance lease.

Despite the fact that the national accounting standards are considered IFRS-based, there are several areas that are missing in the local rules, but that constitute an important part of the IFRS. Particularly, companies are not required to prepare segment reporting, disclose information on governmental subsidies, and disclose the nature of contingent assets and liabilities. It is also uncommon for companies to disclose information about collateral items and test assets for impairment. These and other differences between the national standards and IFRS explain why local accountants were reluctant to fully accept IFRS. Of particular importance is implementation of IFRS among small and medium size enterprises that have limited professional knowledge and technical capabilities to switch to IFRS. Besides, these organizations are typically the last ones to be notified of the modifications in the IFRS standards, therefore struggling to produce accurate information on a timely basis.

Sharipov and Molodtsov (2015) outlined additional problems faced by the accounting community, such as reluctance of professional accounting organizations to be involved in the regulations process, low level of auditors' professionalism, and lack of IFRS-based education. These authors suggest that the national government is now heavily investing in the educational process in order to raise a new generation of specialists (auditors, financial managers, consultants) who would be highly skilled in preparing financial reports in accordance with global practices. Coordination between Kazakh regulatory authorities and those of other, more mature, markets is another important factor for the IFRS adoption success.

In summary, Kazakhstan's path towards becoming one of the most advanced emerging nations, for which it implemented progressive capital market reforms, has had some caveats. Nevertheless, the progress in increasing the level of reporting transparency and attracting foreign capital is indisputable. Importantly, other emerging nations, including Kazakhstan's CIS partners such as Russia, have also implemented progressive reforms and have been recovering from the recent financial crisis at a faster pace than Kazakhstan. At present, significant changes in the regulatory environment and business laws are still required, without doubts, in order for Kazakhstan to be able to keep attracting investor attention and to sustain the positive growth that was achieved in the last two decades.

Chapter 7. Conclusions

I began this book with the citation from the renowned philosopher, Virgil, "We are in for a new century, new times are coming...". Indeed, at the onset of the independence of Kazakhstan, one could hardly imagine the extent of the changes through which the country would journey over just two and a half decades. Some would argue that the painful reforms launched by the national government have not always been understood by the general public and were rather painful for the population that had to sprint through several stages of reforms within a short timeframe. Others would suggest that one thing is certain: Kazakhstan has become an effective state with its own independent history and is placed among the most progressive emerging markets.

In this book I focused only on one aspect of Kazakhstan's development—the changes in the capital market system, of which adoption of International Financial Reporting Standards was a key component. I report the evidence supporting this reform, to the disappointment of the critics who argued that Kazakhstan's rapid adoption of IFRS would be unsuccessful, creating chaos in the reporting environment for years ahead. Importantly, I adopted a novel perspective to analyze Kazakhstan's choice to be the first and early adopter of IFRS, among the CIS states—the resource dependence theory. I believe that this framework provides a unique, unexplored context, to evaluate the rationale behind a nation's decision to adopt IFRS. To my knowledge, this is the first study to undertake such an investigation and the findings reported in the previous chapters are of significant importance to global stakeholders—investors, standard setters, and other emerging nations.

Bibliography

Abdel-khalik, A.R., Wong, K.A., Wu, A., 1999. The information environment of China's A and B shares: Can we make sense of the numbers? The International Journal of Accounting, 34, 467–489.

Abrosimova, N., Dissanaike, G., Linowski, D., 2005. Testing the weak form efficiency of the Russian stock market. Working paper.

Agency of Statistics of the Republic of Kazakhstan. 2016. Retrieved from: www. Stat.gov.kz.

Ahmed, K., Chalmers, K., Khlif, H., 2013. A meta-analysis of IFRS adoption effects. The International Journal of Accounting 48 (2), 173–217.

Alali, F., Foote, P., 2012. The value relevance of International Financial Reporting Standards: empirical evidence in an emerging market. The International Journal of Accounting 47, 175–201.

Alam, MI, Tanweer, H., Kadapakkam, P-R., 1999. An application of variance ratio test to five Asian stock markets. Review of Pacific Basin Financial Markets and Policies 2 (3), 301–315.

Alnodel, A., 2015. Does mandatory IFRS adoption improve market efficiency in emerging stock markets? Evidence from Saudi Arabia. Global Review of Accounting and Finance 6 (2), 1–15.

Alon, A., 2013. Complexity and dual institutionality: The case of IFRS adoption in Russia. Corporate Governance: An International Review 21 (1), 42–57.

Alon, A., Dwyer, P., 2014. Early adoption of IFRS as a strategic response to transnational and local influences. The International Journal of Accounting 49 (4), 348–370.

Amiram, D., 2012. Financial information globalization and foreign investment decisions. Journal of International Accounting Research 11 (2), 57–81.

Ansotegui, A., Bassiouny, A., Tooma, E., 2009. The law of one price in Global Depositary Receipts: Empirical evidence from Egyptian GDRs. Working paper series ESADE.

Armstrong, C., Barth, M., Jagolinzer, A., Riedl, E., 2012. Market reaction to the adoption of IFRS in Europe. The Accounting Review 85(1), 31–61.

Arnold, P.J., 2005. Disciplining domestic regulation: the World Trade Organization and the market for professional services. Accounting, Organizations and Society 30, 299-330.

Ashraf, J., Ghani, W., 2005. Accounting development in Pakistan. The International Journal of Accounting 40: 175–201.

Ayagan, B., Anafinova, M., Abazov, R., 2011. The history of sovereign Kazakhstan: 20 years of independence. Almaty: Rarity.

Ayagan, B., Auanasova, A., Suleymanov, A., 2014. Novejshaya istorija Kazakhstana (1991–2014). Almaty: Atamura.

Ball, R., 1995. Making accounting more international: why, how, and how far will it go? Journal of Applied Corporate Finance 8 (Fall), 19–29.

Ball, R., 2006. International Financial Reporting Standards (IFRS): pros and cons for investors. Accounting and Business Research 36 (Special issue), 5–27.

Ball, R., Kothari, S., Robin, A., 2000. The effect of international institutional factors on properties of accounting earnings. Journal of Accounting and Economics 29, 1–51.

Ball, R., Robin, A., Wu, J., 2003. Incentives versus standards: Properties of accounting income in four East Asian countries. Journal of Accounting and Economics 3, 235–270.

Barth, M., Clinch, G., 2009. Scale effects in capital markets-based accounting research. Journal of Business Finance and Accounting 36 (3), 253–288.

Barth, M., Kallapur, S., 1996. The effects of cross-sectional scale difference on regression results in empirical accounting research. Contemporary Accounting Research 13 (3), 527–567.

Barth, M., Landsman, W., Lang, M., 2008. International accounting standards and accounting quality. Journal of Accounting Research 46(3), 467–498.

Barth, M., Landsman, W., Lang, M., Williams, C., 2012. Are IFRS-based and US GAAP-based accounting amounts comparable? Journal of Accounting and Economics 54, 68–93.

Bartov, E., Goldberg, S., Kim, M., 2005. Comparative value relevance among German, US and International Accounting Standards: A German stock market perspective. Journal of Accounting, Auditing and Finance 20, 95–119.

Berentaev, K., 2001. Suverennij Kazakhstan na rubeje tysjacheletij. Razdel II: Ekonomika Kazakhstana v 90-e gody XX stoletija. Osnovnije etapy ekonomicheskoj politiki. Almaty.

Birnbaum, P., 1985. Political strategies of regulated organizations as functions of context and fear. Strategic Management Journal 6: 135–150.

Blinnikov, M.S., 2011. A geography of Russia and its neighbors. The Guilford Press.

Blumenritt, T., Nigh, D., 2002. The integration of subsidiary political activities in multinational corporations. Journal of International Business Studies 33, 57–77.

Bourmistrov, A., Mellemvik, F., 1999. Russian local governmental reforms: autonomy for Accounting Development? European Accounting Review 8 (4), 675–700.

Bychkova, S., 1996. The development and status of auditing in Russia. European Accounting Review 5 (1), 77–90.

Cannizzaro, A., Weiner, A., 2015. Multinational investment and voluntary disclosure: project-level evidence from the petroleum industry. Accounting, organizations and society 42, 32–47.

Casciaro, T., Piskorski, M., 2005. Power imbalance, mutual dependence, and constraint absorption: A closer look at resource dependence theory. Administrative Science Quarterly 50: 167–199.

Chen, C., Chen, J., Su, S., 2001. Is accounting information value-relevant in the emerging Chinese stock market? Journal of International Accounting, Auditing and Taxation 10, 1–22.

Chen, C., Ding, Y., Xu, B., 2014. Convergence of accounting standards and foreign direct

investment. The International Journal of Accounting 49 (1), 53–86.

Chong, T., Cheng, S., Wong, E., 2010. A comparison of stock market efficiency of the BRIC countries. Technology and Investment 1, 235–238.

Christensen, H., Hail, L., Leuz, C., 2013. Mandatory IFRS reporting and changes in enforcement. Journal of Accounting and Economics 56, 147–177.

Coffee, J., 1999. The future as history: the prospects for global convergence in corporate governance and its implications. North-Western Law Review 93, 641–707.

Dalton, D., Daily, C., Johnson, J., Ellstrand, A., 1999. Number of directors and financial performance: A meta-analysis. Academy of Management Journal 42: 674–686.

Dalton, D., Kesner, I., 1983. Inside/outside succession and organizational size: The pragmatics of executive replacement. Academy of Management Journal 26: 736–742.

Das, S., Sen, P., Sengupta, S., 1998. Impact of strategic alliances on firm valuation. Academy of Management Journal 41: 27–41.

Daske, H., Hail, L., Leuz, C., Verdi, R., 2008. Mandatory IFRS reporting around the world: Early evidence on the economic consequences. Journal of Accounting Research 46, 1085–1142.

Daske, H., Hail, L., Leuz, C, Verdi, R., 2013. Adopting a label: heterogeneity in the economic consequences around IAS/IFRS adoptions. Journal of Accounting Research 51 (3), 495–547.

DiMaggio, P., Powell, W., 1983. The iron cage revisited: Institutional isomorphism and collective rationality in organizational fields. American Sociological Review 48, 147–160.

Djakisheva, U., 2014. Primenenije MSFO v kazakhstanskih predprijatiajh I ee integracija v mirovuju ekonomiku. Vestnik KazNPU. Almaty.

Doupnik, S., 1992. Recent Innovations in German Accounting Practice Through the Integration of EC Directives, Advances in International Accounting 5, 75–103.

Dow Jones Indices, 2016. Retrieved from: http://www.djindexes.com/.

Easton, P., 1998. Discussion of revalued financial, tangible, and intangible assets: association with shares prices and non-market-based value estimates. Journal of Accounting Research 36, 235–247.

Easton, P., Sommers, G., 2003. Scale and the scale effect in market-based accounting research. Journal of Business Finance and Accounting 30 (1), 25–55.

Elg, U., 2000. Firms' home-market relationships: Their role when selecting international alliance partners. Journal of International Business Studies 31, 169–177.

Ernst & Young, 2015/2016. Business environment: Kazakhstan. Retrieved from: http://www.ey.com/KZ/en/Issues/Business-environment/EY-Kazakhstan-attractiveness-survey-2014#.VktxIL-Avv1.

European Commission Directives, 1998/2003. Retrieved from: http://eur-lex.europa.eu/legal-content/EN/TXT/?uri=URISERV%3Al26010.

Fama, E., 1965. Random walks in stock market price. Financial Analysts Journal 21 (5), 55–59.

Federal State Statistics Services of Russia, 2016. Retrieved from: www.gks.ru.

Foerster, S., Karolyi, G., 1999. The effects of market segmentation and investor recognition on asset prices: evidence from foreign stocks listing in the United States. Journal of Finance 54, 981–1013.

Francis, J., Schipper, K., 1999. Have financial statements lost their relevance? Journal of Accounting Research 37, 319–352.

Goldman Sachs Guide to Capital Markets, 2016. Retrieved from: http://www.goldmansachs.com/s/interactive-guide-to-capital-markets/.

Goncharov, I. Zimmermann, J., 2006. Earnings management when incentives compete: The role of tax accounting in Russia. Journal of International Accounting Research 5 (1), 41–65.

Guerreiro, M., Rodrigues, L., Craig, R., 2012. Voluntary adoption of International Financial Reporting Standards by large unlisted companies in Portugal—Institutional logics and strategic responses. Accounting, Organizations and Society 37, 482–499.

Gulati, R., Sytch, M., 2007. Dependence asymmetry and joint dependence in interorganizational relationships: Effects of embeddedness on a manufacturer's performance in procurement relationships. Administrative Science Quarterly 52: 32–69.

Hall, S., Urga, G., 2002. Testing for ongoing efficiency in the Russian stock market. Working Paper.

Harrison, J., Torres, D., Kukalis, S., 1988. The changing of the guard: Turnover and structural change in the top-management positions. Administrative Science Quarterly 33: 211–232.

Hassan, M., 2008. The development of accounting regulations in Egypt: Legitimating the International Accounting Standards. Managerial Auditing Journal 23 (5), 467–484.

Hassan, E., Rankin, M., Lu, W, 2014. The development of accounting regulation in Iraq and the IFRS adoption decision: an institutional perspective. The International Journal of Accounting 49 (4), 371–390.

Hillman, A., Zardkoohi, A., Bierman, L., 1999. Corporate political strategies and firm performance: Indications of firm-specific benefits from. Strategic Management Journal 20, 67–81.

Hillman, A., Withers, M., Collins, B., 2009. Resource dependence theory: A review. Journal of Management 35 (6), 1404–1427.

Hitt, M., Tyler, B., 1991. Strategic decision models: Integrating different perspectives. Strategic Management Journal 12, 327–351.

Hoarau, C., 1995. International accounting harmonization: American hegemony or mutual recognition with benchmarks? European Accounting Review 4 (2), 217–233.

Hope, O., 2003. Disclosure practices, enforcement of accounting standards, and analysts' forecast accuracy: an international study. Journal of Accounting Research 41 (2), 235–272.

Hope, O., Jin, J., Kang, T., 2006. Empirical evidence on jurisdictions that adopt IFRS. Journal of International Accounting Research 5, 1–20.

Hung, M., Subramanyam, K., 2007. Financial statement effects of adopting international accounting standards: the case of Germany. Review of Accounting Studies 12, 623–657.

IAS Plus Deloitte. IFRS adoption by country, 2006/2016). Retrieved from: http://www.iasplus.com/en/resources/ifrs-topics/adoption-of-ifrs.

International Accounting Standards Board (IASB), 2016. Retrieved from: www.iasb.org.

IFRS Foundation Constitution, 2012. Retrieved from: http://www.ifrs.org/The-organisation/Governance-and-accountability/Constitution/Documents/IFRS-Foundation-Constitution-January-2013.pdf.

Johnson, R., Greening, D., 1999. The effects of corporate governance and institutional ownership types of corporate social performance. Academy of Management Journal 42, 564–576.

Joos, P., Lang, M., 1994. The effects of accounting diversity: evidence from the European community. Journal of Accounting Research 32, 141–168.

Judge, W., Li, S., Pinsker, R., 2010. National adoption of International Accounting Standards: An institutional perspective. Corporate Governance: An International Review 18 (3), 161–174.

Karampinis, N., Hevas, D., 2011. Mandating IFRS in an unfavorable environment: the Greek experience. The International Journal of Accounting 46 (3): 304–332.

Kazakhstan Stock Exchange (KASE), 2016. Retrieved from: http://www.kase.kz/en.

Kazakhstan Strategy 2050, 2012. Retrieved from: http://kazakhstan2050.com/.

Kim, O., 2013a. Russian accounting system: value relevance of reported information and the IFRS adoption perspective. The International Journal of Accounting 48 (4), 525–547.

Kim, O., 2013b. The global recognition strategy of blue chips of the Russian and Commonwealth of Independent States (CIS) markets. Journal of Contemporary Accounting and Economics 9 (2), 151–169.

Kim, O., 2016a. The IFRS adoption reform through the lens of neo-institutionalism: The case of the Russian Federation. The International Journal of Accounting 51 (3).

Kim, O., 2016b. Market efficiency and arbitrage opportunities for Russian depositary receipts cross-listed on the London Stock Exchange. Review of Pacific Basin Financial Markets and Policies 19 (2).

Kim, O., Pinnuck, M., 2014. Competition among exchanges through simplified disclosure requirements: Evidence from the American and global depositary receipts. Accounting and Business Research 44 (1), 1–40.

King, N., Beattie, A., Cristescu, A., Weetman, P., 2001. Developing accounting and audit in a transition economy: the Romanian experience. European Accounting Review 10 (1), 149–71.

Kosmala, K., 2005. True and fair view or rzetelny i jasny obraz? A surevy of Polish practitioners. European Accounting Review 14 (3), 579–602.

KPMG in Kazakhstan and Central Asia. Investment Guide, 2013. Retrieved from: https://www.kpmg.com/KZ/ru/IssuesAndInsights/ArticlesAndPublications/Documents/Investment%20guide.pdf.

Kurganbayeva, G., 2009. Ekonomika Kazakhstana v XXI veke. Kazakhstanskij Institut strategicheskih issledovanij pri Presidente RK. Almaty.

La Porta, R., Lopez-de-Silanes, F., Shleifer, A., Vishny, R., 1997. Legal determinants of external finance. Journal of Finance 52 (3), 1131–1150.

La Porta, R., Lopez-de-Silanes, F., Shleifer, A., Vishny, R., 2000. Investor protection and corporate governance. Journal of Financial Economics 58, 3–27.

Lester, R.., Hillman, A., Zardkoohi, A., Cannella, A., 2008. Former government officials as outside directors: The role of human and social capital. Academy of Management Journal 51, 999–1013.

Liu, J., Liu, C., 2007. Value relevance of accounting information in different stock market segments: The case of Chinese A-, B- and H-shares. Journal of International Accounting Research 6, 55–81.

LOC, CIA, EIA, 2013. Understanding Kazakhstan: history, geography and economy. Intercultural Press.

Lomi, A., Pattison, P., 2006. Manufacturing relations: An empirical study of the organization of production across multiple networks. Organization Science 17, 313–332.

Melloni, N., 2006. Market without economy. The 1998 Russian financial crisis. Ibidem-Verlag.

Miller, D., 1999. The market's reaction to international cross-listing: evidence from depositary receipts. Journal of Financial Economics 51, 103–123.

Mitchell, R., Agle, B., Wood, D., 1997. Toward a theory of stakeholder identification and salience: Defining the principle of who and what really counts. Academy of Management Review 22, 853–886.

Mir, M., Rahaman, A., 2005. The adoption of international accounting standards in Bangladesh: an exploration of rationale and process. Accounting, Auditing and Accountability Journal 18 (6), 816-841.

Ministry of Finance of Kazakhstan, 2015. Retrieved from: http://www.minfin.gov.kz/irj/portal/anonymous.

Ministry of Finance of Russia, 2005. Retrieved from: http://government.ru/en/news/.

Morozov, A., 2005. Kazakhstan za gody nezavisimosty. Kazakhstanskij Institut strategicheskih issledovanij pri Presidente RK. Almaty.

Moscow Exchange, 2016. Retrieved from: http://moex.com/en/.

Mullery, R., Agle, B., Perrin, N., 1995. A structural analysis of corporate political activity. Business and Society 34 147–171.

Naranjo, P., Saavedra, D., Verdi, R., 2016. Financial reporting regulation and financing decisions. Working paper series.

Nasdaq, 2016. Retrieved from: http://www.nasdaq.com/investing/glossary/c/capital-market.

National Bank of Kazakhstan, 2016. Archive of announcement. Retrieved from: http://www.nationalbank.kz/.

Nobes, C., 1998. Towards a General Model of the Reasons for International Differences in Financial Reporting Abacus 34 (2), 166.

Nazarbaev, N., 1997. Kazakhstan—2030: Protsvetanije, bezopasnost I uluchshenie blagosostojanija kazakhstantsev. Poslanije narodu Kazakhstana. Adilet. Almaty.

Ohlson, J., 1995. Earnings, book values and dividends in quality valuations. Contemporary Accounting Research 11, 661–688.

Olibe, K., 2016. Security returns and volume responses around International Financial Reporting Standards (IFRS) earnings announcements. The International Journal of Accounting 51 (2), 240–265.

Pearce, J., Zahra, S., 1992. Board composition from a strategic contingency perspective. Journal of Management Studies 29, 411–438.

Palmer, D., Barber, B., 2001. Challengers, elites, and owning families: A social class theory of corporate acquisitions in the 1960s. Administrative Science Quarterly 46, 87–120.

Peng, M., Luo, Y., 2000. Managerial ties and firm performance in a transition economy: The nature of a micro-macro link. Academy of Management Journal 43, 486–501.

Perera, H., Baydoun, N, 2007. Convergence with International Financial Reporting Standards: The Case of Indonesia. Advances in International Accounting 20, 201–224.

Pfeffer, J., 1972. Merger as a response to organizational interdependence. Administrative Science Quarterly 17, 382–394.

Pfeffer, J., 1987. A resource dependence perspective on interorganizational relations. In M.S. Mizruchi, & M. Schwartz (Eds.), Intercorporate relations: The structural analysis of business: 22–25. Cambridge, Cambridge University Press.

Pfeffer, J., Salancik, G., 1978. The external control of organization. Stanford, Stanford University Press.

Prather-Kinsey, J., 2006. Developing countries converging with developed-country accounting standards: Evidence from South Africa and Mexico. The International Journal of Accounting 41, 141–162.

Ramanna, K., Sletten, E., 2016. Network effects in countries' adoption of IFRS. The Accounting Review, Forthcoming.

Richard, J., 1995. The Evolution of the Romanian and Russian Accounting charts after the collapse of the Communist system. European Accounting Review 4, 305–316.

Ritter, J., 1991. The long-run performance of initial public offerings. Journal of Finance 46, 3–27.

Rodrigues, L., Craig, R., 2006. Assessing international accounting harmonization using hegelian dialectic, isomorphism, and Foucault. Critical Perspectives in Accounting 18, 739–757.

Salter, S., Kang, T., Gotti, A., Doupnik, T., 2013. The role of social values, accounting values and institutions in determining accounting conservatism. Management International Review 53 (4), 607–632.

Saudagaran, C., 2009. International accounting: a user perspective. Chicago, CCH Group.

Saudagaran, S., Biddle, G., 2003. Economic integration and accounting harmonization options in emerging markets: Adopting the IASC/IASB model in ASEAN. Research in Accounting in Emerging Economies 5, 239–266.

Schipper, K., 2005. The introduction of International Accounting Standards in Europe: implications for international convergence. European Accounting Review 14 (1), 101–126.

Sharipov, A., Molodstov, E., 2015. Etapy perehoda systemy buhgaltersoko ucheta I finansovoj otchetnosti Respubliki Kazkahstan na MSFO. Young Scientist 8, 23–25.

Schwartz, K., Menon, K., 1985. Executive succession in failing firms. Academy of Management Journal 28, 680–686.

Smirnova, I., Sokolov, J., Emmanuel, C., 199). Accounting education in Russia today. European Accounting Review 4 (4), 833–846.

Sokolov, J., Kovalev, V., 1996. In defense of Russian Accounting: a reply to foreign critics. European Accounting Review 5 (4), 743–762.

Solodchenko, I., Sucher, P., 2005. Accounting in Ukraine since independence: real politik, problems and prospects. European Accounting Review 14 (3), 603–633.

Stearns, T., Hoffman, A., Heide, J., 1987. Performance of commercial television stations as an outcome of interorganizational linkages and environmental conditions. Academy of Management Journal 30, 71–90.

Stiglitz, J., 2002. Globalization and its Discontents. New York, Norton.

Stulz, R., 1999. Globalization, corporate finance, and the cost of capital. Journal of Applied

Corporate Finance 12, 8–25.

Sucher, P., Bychkova, S., 2001. Auditor independence in economies in transition: a study of Russia. European Accounting Review 10(4), 817–841.

The International Monetary Fund, World economic outlook, 2013/2015. Retrieved from: http://www.econstats.com/weo/CRUS.htm.

The US Department of State, 2015. Country profile: Kazakhstan. Retrieved from: http://www.state.gov/outofdate/bgn/kazakhstan/47484.htm.

The World Bank, 2013/2016. Country profile: Kazakhstan. Retrieved from: http://www.worldbank.org/en/country/kazakhstan/research.

The World Bank, World Development Indicators, 2015. Retrieved from: http://data.worldbank.org/data-catalog/world-development-indicators.

Thiele, T., 2014. Multiscaling and stock market efficiency in China. Review of Pacific Basin Financial Markets and Policies 17 (4).

Timoshenko, K., 2010. Russian government accounting: Changes at the central level and at a university. VDM Verlag Dr. Mülle.

Touron, P., 2005. The adoption of US GAAP by French firms before the creation of the International Accounting Standard Committee: an institutional explanation. Critical Perspectives on Accounting 16, 851–873.

Tyrrall, D., Woodward, D., Rakhimbekova, A., 2007. The relevance of International Financial Reporting Standards to a developing country: Evidence from Kazakhstan. The International Journal of Accounting 42, 82–110.

Uddin, S., Tsamenyi, M., 2005. Public sector reforms and the public interest. Accounting, Auditing and Accountability Journal 18 (5), 648–674.

Urich, D. Barney, J., 1984. Perspectives in organizations: Resource dependence, efficiency, and population. Academy of Management Review 9, 471–481.

USAID Country profile—Kazakhstan, 2015. Retrieved from: https://www.usaid.gov/kazakhstan.

Walter, G., Barney, J., 1990. Management objectives in mergers and acquisitions. Strategic Management Journal 11, 79–86.

Weetman, P., 2006. Discovering the "international" in accounting and finance. The British Accounting Review 38, 351–370.

Wiener Börse Major Indices, 2016. Retrieved from: http://en.wiener borse.at/indices/.

World Economic Forum, 2016. Global Competitiveness report. Retrieved from: www.weforum.org.

World Federation of Exchanges, 2016. Retrieved from: http://www.world-exchanges.org/home/.

Zhang, Y., 2006. The presence of a separate COO/president and its impact on strategic change and CEO dismissal. Strategic Management Journal 27, 283–300.

SOVIET AND POST-SOVIET POLITICS AND SOCIETY

Edited by Dr. Andreas Umland

ISSN 1614-3515

1 *Андреас Умланд (ред.)*
Воплощение Европейской
конвенции по правам человека в
России
Философские, юридические и
эмпирические исследования
ISBN 3-89821-387-0

2 *Christian Wipperfürth*
Russland – ein vertrauenswürdiger
Partner?
Grundlagen, Hintergründe und Praxis
gegenwärtiger russischer Außenpolitik
Mit einem Vorwort von Heinz Timmermann
ISBN 3-89821-401-X

3 *Manja Hussner*
Die Übernahme internationalen Rechts
in die russische und deutsche
Rechtsordnung
Eine vergleichende Analyse zur
Völkerrechtsfreundlichkeit der Verfassungen
der Russländischen Föderation und der
Bundesrepublik Deutschland
Mit einem Vorwort von Rainer Arnold
ISBN 3-89821-438-9

4 *Matthew Tejada*
Bulgaria's Democratic Consolidation
and the Kozloduy Nuclear Power Plant
(KNPP)
The Unattainability of Closure
With a foreword by Richard J. Crampton
ISBN 3-89821-439-7

5 *Марк Григорьевич Меерович*
Квадратные метры, определяющие
сознание
Государственная жилищная политика в
СССР. 1921 – 1941 гг
ISBN 3-89821-474-5

6 *Andrei P. Tsygankov, Pavel
A. Tsygankov (Eds.)*
New Directions in Russian
International Studies
ISBN 3-89821-422-2

7 *Марк Григорьевич Меерович*
Как власть народ к труду приучала
Жилище в СССР – средство управления
людьми. 1917 – 1941 гг.
С предисловием Елены Осокиной
ISBN 3-89821-495-8

8 *David J. Galbreath*
Nation-Building and Minority Politics
in Post-Socialist States
Interests, Influence and Identities in Estonia
and Latvia
With a foreword by David J. Smith
ISBN 3-89821-467-2

9 *Алексей Юрьевич Безугольный*
Народы Кавказа в Вооруженных
силах СССР в годы Великой
Отечественной войны 1941-1945 гг.
С предисловием Николая Бугая
ISBN 3-89821-475-3

10 *Вячеслав Лихачев и Владимир
Прибыловский (ред.)*
Русское Национальное Единство,
1990-2000. В 2-х томах
ISBN 3-89821-523-7

11 *Николай Бугай (ред.)*
Народы стран Балтии в условиях
сталинизма (1940-е – 1950-е годы)
Документированная история
ISBN 3-89821-525-3

12 *Ingmar Bredies (Hrsg.)*
Zur Anatomie der Orange Revolution
in der Ukraine
Wechsel des Elitenregimes oder Triumph des
Parlamentarismus?
ISBN 3-89821-524-5

13 *Anastasia V. Mitrofanova*
The Politicization of Russian
Orthodoxy
Actors and Ideas
With a foreword by William C. Gay
ISBN 3-89821-481-8

14 Nathan D. Larson
Alexander Solzhenitsyn and the
Russo-Jewish Question
ISBN 3-89821-483-4

15 Guido Houben
Kulturpolitik und Ethnizität
Staatliche Kunstförderung im Russland der neunziger Jahre
Mit einem Vorwort von Gert Weisskirchen
ISBN 3-89821-542-3

16 Leonid Luks
Der russische „Sonderweg"?
Aufsätze zur neuesten Geschichte Russlands im europäischen Kontext
ISBN 3-89821-496-6

17 Евгений Мороз
История «Мёртвой воды» – от страшной сказки к большой политике
Политическое неоязычество в постсоветской России
ISBN 3-89821-551-2

18 Александр Верховский и Галина Кожевникова (ред.)
Этническая и религиозная интолерантность в российских СМИ
Результаты мониторинга 2001-2004 гг.
ISBN 3-89821-569-5

19 Christian Ganzer
Sowjetisches Erbe und ukrainische Nation
Das Museum der Geschichte des Zaporoger Kosakentums auf der Insel Chortycja
Mit einem Vorwort von Frank Golczewski
ISBN 3-89821-504-0

20 Эльза-Баир Гучинова
Помнить нельзя забыть
Антропология депортационной травмы калмыков
С предисловием Кэролайн Хамфри
ISBN 3-89821-506-7

21 Юлия Лидерман
Мотивы «проверки» и «испытания» в постсоветской культуре
Советское прошлое в российском кинематографе 1990-х годов
С предисловием Евгения Марголита
ISBN 3-89821-511-3

22 Tanya Lokshina, Ray Thomas, Mary Mayer (Eds.)
The Imposition of a Fake Political Settlement in the Northern Caucasus
The 2003 Chechen Presidential Election
ISBN 3-89821-436-2

23 Timothy McCajor Hall, Rosie Read (Eds.)
Changes in the Heart of Europe
Recent Ethnographies of Czechs, Slovaks, Roma, and Sorbs
With an afterword by Zdeněk Salzmann
ISBN 3-89821-606-3

24 Christian Autengruber
Die politischen Parteien in Bulgarien und Rumänien
Eine vergleichende Analyse seit Beginn der 90er Jahre
Mit einem Vorwort von Dorothée de Nève
ISBN 3-89821-476-1

25 Annette Freyberg-Inan with Radu Cristescu
The Ghosts in Our Classrooms, or: John Dewey Meets Ceauşescu
The Promise and the Failures of Civic Education in Romania
ISBN 3-89821-416-8

26 John B. Dunlop
The 2002 Dubrovka and 2004 Beslan Hostage Crises
A Critique of Russian Counter-Terrorism
With a foreword by Donald N. Jensen
ISBN 3-89821-608-X

27 Peter Koller
Das touristische Potenzial von Kam''janec'–Podil's'kyj
Eine fremdenverkehrsgeographische Untersuchung der Zukunftsperspektiven und Maßnahmenplanung zur Destinationsentwicklung des „ukrainischen Rothenburg"
Mit einem Vorwort von Kristiane Klemm
ISBN 3-89821-640-3

28 Françoise Daucé, Elisabeth Sieca-Kozlowski (Eds.)
Dedovshchina in the Post-Soviet Military
Hazing of Russian Army Conscripts in a Comparative Perspective
With a foreword by Dale Herspring
ISBN 3-89821-616-0

29	Florian Strasser Zivilgesellschaftliche Einflüsse auf die Orange Revolution Die gewaltlose Massenbewegung und die ukrainische Wahlkrise 2004 Mit einem Vorwort von Egbert Jahn ISBN 3-89821-648-9	36	Sebastian Schlegel Der „Weiße Archipel" Sowjetische Atomstädte 1945-1991 Mit einem Geleitwort von Thomas Bohn ISBN 3-89821-679-9
30	Rebecca S. Katz The Georgian Regime Crisis of 2003-2004 A Case Study in Post-Soviet Media Representation of Politics, Crime and Corruption ISBN 3-89821-413-3	37	Vyacheslav Likhachev Political Anti-Semitism in Post-Soviet Russia Actors and Ideas in 1991-2003 Edited and translated from Russian by Eugene Veklerov ISBN 3-89821-529-6
31	Vladimir Kantor Willkür oder Freiheit Beiträge zur russischen Geschichtsphilosophie Ediert von Dagmar Herrmann sowie mit einem Vorwort versehen von Leonid Luks ISBN 3-89821-589-X	38	Josette Baer (Ed.) Preparing Liberty in Central Europe Political Texts from the Spring of Nations 1848 to the Spring of Prague 1968 With a foreword by Zdeněk V. David ISBN 3-89821-546-6
32	Laura A. Victoir The Russian Land Estate Today A Case Study of Cultural Politics in Post-Soviet Russia With a foreword by Priscilla Roosevelt ISBN 3-89821-426-5	39	Михаил Лукьянов Российский консерватизм и реформа, 1907-1914 С предисловием Марка Д. Стейнберга ISBN 3-89821-503-2
33	Ivan Katchanovski Cleft Countries Regional Political Divisions and Cultures in Post-Soviet Ukraine and Moldova With a foreword by Francis Fukuyama ISBN 3-89821-558-X	40	Nicola Melloni Market Without Economy The 1998 Russian Financial Crisis With a foreword by Eiji Furukawa ISBN 3-89821-407-9
34	Florian Mühlfried Postsowjetische Feiern Das Georgische Bankett im Wandel Mit einem Vorwort von Kevin Tuite ISBN 3-89821-601-2	41	Dmitrij Chmelnizki Die Architektur Stalins Bd. 1: Studien zu Ideologie und Stil Bd. 2: Bilddokumentation Mit einem Vorwort von Bruno Flierl ISBN 3-89821-515-6
35	Roger Griffin, Werner Loh, Andreas Umland (Eds.) Fascism Past and Present, West and East An International Debate on Concepts and Cases in the Comparative Study of the Extreme Right With an afterword by Walter Laqueur ISBN 3-89821-674-8	42	Katja Yafimava Post-Soviet Russian-Belarussian Relationships The Role of Gas Transit Pipelines With a foreword by Jonathan P. Stern ISBN 3-89821-655-1
		43	Boris Chavkin Verflechtungen der deutschen und russischen Zeitgeschichte Aufsätze und Archivfunde zu den Beziehungen Deutschlands und der Sowjetunion von 1917 bis 1991 Ediert von Markus Edlinger sowie mit einem Vorwort versehen von Leonid Luks ISBN 3-89821-756-6

44 *Anastasija Grynenko in Zusammenarbeit mit Claudia Dathe*
Die Terminologie des Gerichtswesens der Ukraine und Deutschlands im Vergleich
Eine übersetzungswissenschaftliche Analyse juristischer Fachbegriffe im Deutschen, Ukrainischen und Russischen
Mit einem Vorwort von Ulrich Hartmann
ISBN 3-89821-691-8

45 *Anton Burkov*
The Impact of the European Convention on Human Rights on Russian Law
Legislation and Application in 1996-2006
With a foreword by Françoise Hampson
ISBN 978-3-89821-639-5

46 *Stina Torjesen, Indra Overland (Eds.)*
International Election Observers in Post-Soviet Azerbaijan
Geopolitical Pawns or Agents of Change?
ISBN 978-3-89821-743-9

47 *Taras Kuzio*
Ukraine – Crimea – Russia
Triangle of Conflict
ISBN 978-3-89821-761-3

48 *Claudia Šabić*
"Ich erinnere mich nicht, aber L'viv!"
Zur Funktion kultureller Faktoren für die Institutionalisierung und Entwicklung einer ukrainischen Region
Mit einem Vorwort von Melanie Tatur
ISBN 978-3-89821-752-1

49 *Marlies Bilz*
Tatarstan in der Transformation
Nationaler Diskurs und Politische Praxis 1988-1994
Mit einem Vorwort von Frank Golczewski
ISBN 978-3-89821-722-4

50 *Марлен Ларюэль (ред.)*
Современные интерпретации русского национализма
ISBN 978-3-89821-795-8

51 *Sonja Schüler*
Die ethnische Dimension der Armut
Roma im postsozialistischen Rumänien
Mit einem Vorwort von Anton Sterbling
ISBN 978-3-89821-776-7

52 *Галина Кожевникова*
Радикальный национализм в России и противодействие ему
Сборник докладов Центра «Сова» за 2004-2007 гг.
С предисловием Александра Верховского
ISBN 978-3-89821-721-7

53 *Галина Кожевникова и Владимир Прибыловский*
Российская власть в биографиях I
Высшие должностные лица РФ в 2004 г.
ISBN 978-3-89821-796-5

54 *Галина Кожевникова и Владимир Прибыловский*
Российская власть в биографиях II
Члены Правительства РФ в 2004 г.
ISBN 978-3-89821-797-2

55 *Галина Кожевникова и Владимир Прибыловский*
Российская власть в биографиях III
Руководители федеральных служб и агентств РФ в 2004 г.
ISBN 978-3-89821-798-9

56 *Ileana Petroniu*
Privatisierung in Transformationsökonomien
Determinanten der Restrukturierungs-Bereitschaft am Beispiel Polens, Rumäniens und der Ukraine
Mit einem Vorwort von Rainer W. Schäfer
ISBN 978-3-89821-790-3

57 *Christian Wipperfürth*
Russland und seine GUS-Nachbarn
Hintergründe, aktuelle Entwicklungen und Konflikte in einer ressourcenreichen Region
ISBN 978-3-89821-801-6

58 *Togzhan Kassenova*
From Antagonism to Partnership
The Uneasy Path of the U.S.-Russian Cooperative Threat Reduction
With a foreword by Christoph Bluth
ISBN 978-3-89821-707-1

59 *Alexander Höllwerth*
Das sakrale eurasische Imperium des Aleksandr Dugin
Eine Diskursanalyse zum postsowjetischen russischen Rechtsextremismus
Mit einem Vorwort von Dirk Uffelmann
ISBN 978-3-89821-813-9

60   Олег Рябов
     «Россия-Матушка»
     Национализм, гендер и война в России XX
     века
     С предисловием Елены Гощило
     ISBN 978-3-89821-487-2

61   Ivan Maistrenko
     Borot'bism
     A Chapter in the History of the Ukrainian
     Revolution
     With a new introduction by Chris Ford
     Translated by George S. N. Luckyj with the
     assistance of Ivan L. Rudnytsky
     ISBN 978-3-89821-697-5

62   Maryna Romanets
     Anamorphosic Texts and
     Reconfigured Visions
     Improvised Traditions in Contemporary
     Ukrainian and Irish Literature
     ISBN 978-3-89821-576-3

63   Paul D'Anieri and Taras Kuzio (Eds.)
     Aspects of the Orange Revolution I
     Democratization and Elections in Post-
     Communist Ukraine
     ISBN 978-3-89821-698-2

64   Bohdan Harasymiw in collaboration
     with Oleh S. Ilnytzkyj (Eds.)
     Aspects of the Orange Revolution II
     Information and Manipulation Strategies in
     the 2004 Ukrainian Presidential Elections
     ISBN 978-3-89821-699-9

65   Ingmar Bredies, Andreas Umland and
     Valentin Yakushik (Eds.)
     Aspects of the Orange Revolution III
     The Context and Dynamics of the 2004
     Ukrainian Presidential Elections
     ISBN 978-3-89821-803-0

66   Ingmar Bredies, Andreas Umland and
     Valentin Yakushik (Eds.)
     Aspects of the Orange Revolution IV
     Foreign Assistance and Civic Action in the
     2004 Ukrainian Presidential Elections
     ISBN 978-3-89821-808-5

67   Ingmar Bredies, Andreas Umland and
     Valentin Yakushik (Eds.)
     Aspects of the Orange Revolution V
     Institutional Observation Reports on the 2004
     Ukrainian Presidential Elections
     ISBN 978-3-89821-809-2

68   Taras Kuzio (Ed.)
     Aspects of the Orange Revolution VI
     Post-Communist Democratic Revolutions in
     Comparative Perspective
     ISBN 978-3-89821-820-7

69   Tim Bohse
     Autoritarismus statt Selbstverwaltung
     Die Transformation der kommunalen Politik
     in der Stadt Kaliningrad 1990-2005
     Mit einem Geleitwort von Stefan Troebst
     ISBN 978-3-89821-782-8

70   David Rupp
     Die Rußländische Föderation und die
     russischsprachige Minderheit in
     Lettland
     Eine Fallstudie zur Anwaltspolitik Moskaus
     gegenüber den russophonen Minderheiten im
     „Nahen Ausland" von 1991 bis 2002
     Mit einem Vorwort von Helmut Wagner
     ISBN 978-3-89821-778-1

71   Taras Kuzio
     Theoretical and Comparative
     Perspectives on Nationalism
     New Directions in Cross-Cultural and Post-
     Communist Studies
     With a foreword by Paul Robert Magocsi
     ISBN 978-3-89821-815-3

72   Christine Teichmann
     Die Hochschultransformation im
     heutigen Osteuropa
     Kontinuität und Wandel bei der Entwicklung
     des postkommunistischen Universitätswesens
     Mit einem Vorwort von Oskar Anweiler
     ISBN 978-3-89821-842-9

73   Julia Kusznir
     Der politische Einfluss von
     Wirtschaftseliten in russischen
     Regionen
     Eine Analyse am Beispiel der Erdöl- und
     Erdgasindustrie, 1992-2005
     Mit einem Vorwort von Wolfgang Eichwede
     ISBN 978-3-89821-821-4

74   Alena Vysotskaya
     Russland, Belarus und die EU-
     Osterweiterung
     Zur Minderheitenfrage und zum Problem der
     Freizügigkeit des Personenverkehrs
     Mit einem Vorwort von Katlijn Malfliet
     ISBN 978-3-89821-822-1

75   Heiko Pleines (Hrsg.)
     Corporate Governance in post-
     sozialistischen Volkswirtschaften
     ISBN 978-3-89821-766-8

76   Stefan Ihrig
     Wer sind die Moldawier?
     Rumänismus versus Moldowanismus in
     Historiographie und Schulbüchern der
     Republik Moldova, 1991-2006
     Mit einem Vorwort von Holm Sundhaussen
     ISBN 978-3-89821-466-7

77   Galina Kozhevnikova in collaboration
     with Alexander Verkhovsky and
     Eugene Veklerov
     Ultra-Nationalism and Hate Crimes in
     Contemporary Russia
     The 2004-2006 Annual Reports of Moscow's
     SOVA Center
     With a foreword by Stephen D. Shenfield
     ISBN 978-3-89821-868-9

78   Florian Küchler
     The Role of the European Union in
     Moldova's Transnistria Conflict
     With a foreword by Christopher Hill
     ISBN 978-3-89821-850-4

79   Bernd Rechel
     The Long Way Back to Europe
     Minority Protection in Bulgaria
     With a foreword by Richard Crampton
     ISBN 978-3-89821-863-4

80   Peter W. Rodgers
     Nation, Region and History in Post-
     Communist Transitions
     Identity Politics in Ukraine, 1991-2006
     With a foreword by Vera Tolz
     ISBN 978-3-89821-903-7

81   Stephanie Solywoda
     The Life and Work of
     Semen L. Frank
     A Study of Russian Religious Philosophy
     With a foreword by Philip Walters
     ISBN 978-3-89821-457-5

82   Vera Sokolova
     Cultural Politics of Ethnicity
     Discourses on Roma in Communist
     Czechoslovakia
     ISBN 978-3-89821-864-1

83   Natalya Shevchik Ketenci
     Kazakhstani Enterprises in Transition
     The Role of Historical Regional Development
     in Kazakhstan's Post-Soviet Economic
     Transformation
     ISBN 978-3-89821-831-3

84   Martin Malek, Anna Schor-
     Tschudnowskaja (Hrsg.)
     Europa im Tschetschenienkrieg
     Zwischen politischer Ohnmacht und
     Gleichgültigkeit
     Mit einem Vorwort von Lipchan Basajewa
     ISBN 978-3-89821-676-0

85   Stefan Meister
     Das postsowjetische Universitätswesen
     zwischen nationalem und
     internationalem Wandel
     Die Entwicklung der regionalen Hochschule
     in Russland als Gradmesser der
     Systemtransformation
     Mit einem Vorwort von Joan DeBardeleben
     ISBN 978-3-89821-891-7

86   Konstantin Sheiko in collaboration
     with Stephen Brown
     Nationalist Imaginings of the
     Russian Past
     Anatolii Fomenko and the Rise of Alternative
     History in Post-Communist Russia
     With a foreword by Donald Ostrowski
     ISBN 978-3-89821-915-0

87   Sabine Jenni
     Wie stark ist das „Einige Russland"?
     Zur Parteibindung der Eliten und zum
     Wahlerfolg der Machtpartei
     im Dezember 2007
     Mit einem Vorwort von Klaus Armingeon
     ISBN 978-3-89821-961-7

88   Thomas Borén
     Meeting-Places of Transformation
     Urban Identity, Spatial Representations and
     Local Politics in Post-Soviet St Petersburg
     ISBN 978-3-89821-739-2

89   Aygul Ashirova
     Stalinismus und Stalin-Kult in
     Zentralasien
     Turkmenistan 1924-1953
     Mit einem Vorwort von Leonid Luks
     ISBN 978-3-89821-987-7

90 Leonid Luks
   Freiheit oder imperiale Größe?
   Essays zu einem russischen Dilemma
   ISBN 978-3-8382-0011-8

91 Christopher Gilley
   The 'Change of Signposts' in the
   Ukrainian Emigration
   A Contribution to the History of
   Sovietophilism in the 1920s
   With a foreword by Frank Golczewski
   ISBN 978-3-89821-965-5

92 Philipp Casula, Jeronim Perovic
   (Eds.)
   Identities and Politics
   During the Putin Presidency
   The Discursive Foundations of Russia's
   Stability
   With a foreword by Heiko Haumann
   ISBN 978-3-8382-0015-6

93 Marcel Viëtor
   Europa und die Frage
   nach seinen Grenzen im Osten
   Zur Konstruktion ‚europäischer Identität' in
   Geschichte und Gegenwart
   Mit einem Vorwort von Albrecht Lehmann
   ISBN 978-3-8382-0045-3

94 Ben Hellman, Andrei Rogachevskii
   Filming the Unfilmable
   Casper Wrede's 'One Day in the Life
   of Ivan Denisovich'
   Second, Revised and Expanded Edition
   ISBN 978-3-8382-0044-6

95 Eva Fuchslocher
   Vaterland, Sprache, Glaube
   Orthodoxie und Nationenbildung
   am Beispiel Georgiens
   Mit einem Vorwort von Christina von Braun
   ISBN 978-3-89821-884-9

96 Vladimir Kantor
   Das Westlertum und der Weg
   Russlands
   Zur Entwicklung der russischen Literatur und
   Philosophie
   Ediert von Dagmar Herrmann
   Mit einem Beitrag von Nikolaus Lobkowicz
   ISBN 978-3-8382-0102-3

97 Kamran Musayev
   Die postsowjetische Transformation
   im Baltikum und Südkaukasus
   Eine vergleichende Untersuchung der
   politischen Entwicklung Lettlands und
   Aserbaidschans 1985-2009
   Mit einem Vorwort von Leonid Luks
   Ediert von Sandro Henschel
   ISBN 978-3-8382-0103-0

98 Tatiana Zhurzhenko
   Borderlands into Bordered Lands
   Geopolitics of Identity in Post-Soviet Ukraine
   With a foreword by Dieter Segert
   ISBN 978-3-8382-0042-2

99 Кирилл Галушко, Лидия Смола
   (ред.)
   Пределы падения – варианты
   украинского будущего
   Аналитико-прогностические исследования
   ISBN 978-3-8382-0148-1

100 Michael Minkenberg (ed.)
   Historical Legacies and the Radical
   Right in Post-Cold War Central and
   Eastern Europe
   With an afterword by Sabrina P. Ramet
   ISBN 978-3-8382-0124-5

101 David-Emil Wickström
   Rocking St. Petersburg
   Transcultural Flows and Identity Politics in
   the St. Petersburg Popular Music Scene
   With a foreword by Yngvar B. Steinholt
   Second, Revised and Expanded Edition
   ISBN 978-3-8382-0100-9

102 Eva Zabka
   Eine neue „Zeit der Wirren"?
   Der spät- und postsowjetische Systemwandel
   1985-2000 im Spiegel russischer
   gesellschaftspolitischer Diskurse
   Mit einem Vorwort von Margareta Mommsen
   ISBN 978-3-8382-0161-0

103 Ulrike Ziemer
   Ethnic Belonging, Gender and
   Cultural Practices
   Youth Identitites in Contemporary Russia
   With a foreword by Anoop Nayak
   ISBN 978-3-8382-0152-8

104 Ksenia Chepikova
    ,Einiges Russland' - eine zweite
    KPdSU?
    Aspekte der Identitätskonstruktion einer
    postsowjetischen „Partei der Macht"
    Mit einem Vorwort von Torsten Oppelland
    ISBN 978-3-8382-0311-9

105 Леонид Люкс
    Западничество или евразийство?
    Демократия или идеократия?
    Сборник статей об исторических дилеммах
    России
    С предисловием Владимира Кантора
    ISBN 978-3-8382-0211-2

106 Anna Dost
    Das russische Verfassungsrecht auf dem
    Weg zum Föderalismus und zurück
    Zum Konflikt von Rechtsnormen und
    -wirklichkeit in der Russländischen Föderation
    von 1991 bis 2009
    Mit einem Vorwort von Alexander Blankenagel
    ISBN 978-3-8382-0292-1

107 Philipp Herzog
    Sozialistische Völkerfreundschaft,
    nationaler Widerstand oder harmloser
    Zeitvertreib?
    Zur politischen Funktion der Volkskunst
    im sowjetischen Estland
    Mit einem Vorwort von Andreas Kappeler
    ISBN 978-3-8382-0216-7

108 Marlène Laruelle (ed.)
    Russian Nationalism, Foreign Policy,
    and Identity Debates in Putin's Russia
    New Ideological Patterns after the Orange
    Revolution
    ISBN 978-3-8382-0325-6

109 Michail Logvinov
    Russlands Kampf gegen den
    internationalen Terrorismus
    Eine kritische Bestandsaufnahme des
    Bekämpfungsansatzes
    Mit einem Geleitwort von
    Hans-Henning Schröder
    und einem Vorwort von Eckhard Jesse
    ISBN 978-3-8382-0329-4

110 John B. Dunlop
    The Moscow Bombings
    of September 1999
    Examinations of Russian Terrorist Attacks
    at the Onset of Vladimir Putin's Rule
    Second, Revised and Expanded Edition
    ISBN 978-3-8382-0388-1

111 Андрей А. Ковалёв
    Свидетельство из-за кулис
    российской политики I
    Можно ли делать добро из зла?
    (Воспоминания и размышления о
    последних советских и первых
    послесоветских годах)
    With a foreword by Peter Reddaway
    ISBN 978-3-8382-0302-7

112 Андрей А. Ковалёв
    Свидетельство из-за кулис
    российской политики II
    Угроза для себя и окружающих
    (Наблюдения и предостережения
    относительно происходящего после 2000 г.)
    ISBN 978-3-8382-0303-4

113 Bernd Kappenberg
    Zeichen setzen für Europa
    Der Gebrauch europäischer lateinischer
    Sonderzeichen in der deutschen Öffentlichkeit
    Mit einem Vorwort von Peter Schlobinski
    ISBN 978-3-89821-749-1

114 Ivo Mijnssen
    The Quest for an Ideal Youth in
    Putin's Russia I
    Back to Our Future! History, Modernity, and
    Patriotism according to Nashi, 2005-2013
    With a foreword by Jeronim Perović
    Second, Revised and Expanded Edition
    ISBN 978-3-8382-0368-3

115 Jussi Lassila
    The Quest for an Ideal Youth in
    Putin's Russia II
    The Search for Distinctive Conformism in the
    Political Communication of Nashi, 2005-2009
    With a foreword by Kirill Postoutenko
    Second, Revised and Expanded Edition
    ISBN 978-3-8382-0415-4

116 Valerio Trabandt
    Neue Nachbarn, gute Nachbarschaft?
    Die EU als internationaler Akteur am Beispiel
    ihrer Demokratieförderung in Belarus und der
    Ukraine 2004-2009
    Mit einem Vorwort von Jutta Joachim
    ISBN 978-3-8382-0437-6

117 Fabian Pfeiffer
Estlands Außen- und Sicherheitspolitik I
Der estnische Atlantizismus nach der
wiedererlangten Unabhängigkeit 1991-2004
Mit einem Vorwort von Helmut Hubel
ISBN 978-3-8382-0127-6

118 Jana Podßuweit
Estlands Außen- und Sicherheitspolitik II
Handlungsoptionen eines Kleinstaates im
Rahmen seiner EU-Mitgliedschaft (2004-2008)
Mit einem Vorwort von Helmut Hubel
ISBN 978-3-8382-0440-6

119 Karin Pointner
Estlands Außen- und Sicherheitspolitik III
Eine gedächtnispolitische Analyse estnischer
Entwicklungskooperation 2006-2010
Mit einem Vorwort von Karin Liebhart
ISBN 978-3-8382-0435-2

120 Ruslana Vovk
Die Offenheit der ukrainischen
Verfassung für das Völkerrecht und
die europäische Integration
Mit einem Vorwort von Alexander
Blankenagel
ISBN 978-3-8382-0481-9

121 Mykhaylo Banakh
Die Relevanz der Zivilgesellschaft
bei den postkommunistischen
Transformationsprozessen in mittel-
und osteuropäischen Ländern
Das Beispiel der spät- und postsowjetischen
Ukraine 1986-2009
Mit einem Vorwort von Gerhard Simon
ISBN 978-3-8382-0499-4

122 Michael Moser
Language Policy and the Discourse on
Languages in Ukraine under President
Viktor Yanukovych (25 February
2010–28 October 2012)
ISBN 978-3-8382-0497-0 (Paperback edition)
ISBN 978-3-8382-0507-6 (Hardcover edition)

123 Nicole Krome
Russischer Netzwerkkapitalismus
Restrukturierungsprozesse in der
Russischen Föderation am Beispiel des
Luftfahrtunternehmens "Aviastar"
Mit einem Vorwort von Petra Stykow
ISBN 978-3-8382-0534-2

124 David R. Marples
'Our Glorious Past'
Lukashenka's Belarus and
the Great Patriotic War
ISBN 978-3-8382-0574-8 (Paperback edition)
ISBN 978-3-8382-0675-2 (Hardcover edition)

125 Ulf Walther
Russlands "neuer Adel"
Die Macht des Geheimdienstes von
Gorbatschow bis Putin
Mit einem Vorwort von Hans-Georg Wieck
ISBN 978-3-8382-0584-7

126 Simon Geissbühler (Hrsg.)
Kiew – Revolution 3.0
Der Euromaidan 2013/14 und die
Zukunftsperspektiven der Ukraine
ISBN 978-3-8382-0581-6 (Paperback edition)
ISBN 978-3-8382-0681-3 (Hardcover edition)

127 Andrey Makarychev
Russia and the EU
in a Multipolar World
Discourses, Identities, Norms
With a foreword by Klaus Segbers
ISBN 978-3-8382-0629-5

128 Roland Scharff
Kasachstan als postsowjetischer
Wohlfahrtsstaat
Die Transformation des sozialen
Schutzsystems
Mit einem Vorwort von Joachim Ahrens
ISBN 978-3-8382-0622-6

129 Katja Grupp
Bild Lücke Deutschland
Kaliningrader Studierende sprechen über
Deutschland
Mit einem Vorwort von Martin Schulz
ISBN 978-3-8382-0552-6

130 Konstantin Sheiko, Stephen Brown
History as Therapy
Alternative History and Nationalist
Imaginings in Russia, 1991-2014
ISBN 978-3-8382-0665-3

131 Elisa Kriza
Alexander Solzhenitsyn: Cold War
Icon, Gulag Author, Russian
Nationalist?
A Study of the Western Reception of his
Literary Writings, Historical Interpretations,
and Political Ideas
With a foreword by Andrei Rogatchevski
ISBN 978-3-8382-0589-2 (Paperback edition)
ISBN 978-3-8382-0690-5 (Hardcover edition)

Soviet and Post-Soviet Politics and Society (SPPS) Vol. 167
ISSN 1614-3515

General Editor: Andreas Umland,
Institute for Euro-Atlantic Cooperation, Kyiv, umland@stanfordalumni.org

Commissioning Editor: Max Jakob Horstmann,
London, mjh@ibidem.eu

EDITORIAL COMMITTEE*

DOMESTIC & COMPARATIVE POLITICS
Prof. **Ellen Bos**, *Andrássy University of Budapest*
Dr. **Ingmar Bredies**, *FH Bund, Brühl*
Dr. **Andrey Kazantsev**, *MGIMO (U) MID RF, Moscow*
Prof. **Heiko Pleines**, *University of Bremen*
Prof. **Richard Sakwa**, *University of Kent at Canterbury*
Dr. **Sarah Whitmore**, *Oxford Brookes University*
Dr. **Harald Wydra**, *University of Cambridge*

SOCIETY, CLASS & ETHNICITY
Col. **David Glantz**, *"Journal of Slavic Military Studies"*
Dr. **Marlène Laruelle**, *George Washington University*
Dr. **Stephen Shulman**, *Southern Illinois University*
Prof. **Stefan Troebst**, *University of Leipzig*

POLITICAL ECONOMY & PUBLIC POLICY
Prof. em. **Marshall Goldman**, *Wellesley College, Mass.*
Dr. **Andreas Goldthau**, *Central European University*
Dr. **Robert Kravchuk**, *University of North Carolina*
Dr. **David Lane**, *University of Cambridge*
Dr. **Carol Leonard**, *Higher School of Economics, Moscow*
Dr. **Maria Popova**, *McGill University, Montreal*

FOREIGN POLICY & INTERNATIONAL AFFAIRS
Dr. **Peter Duncan**, *University College London*
Prof. **Andreas Heinemann-Grüder**, *University of Bonn*
Dr. **Taras Kuzio**, *Johns Hopkins University*
Prof. **Gerhard Mangott**, *University of Innsbruck*
Dr. **Diana Schmidt-Pfister**, *University of Konstanz*
Dr. **Lisbeth Tarlow**, *Harvard University, Cambridge*
Dr. **Christian Wipperfürth**, *N-Ost Network, Berlin*
Dr. **William Zimmerman**, *University of Michigan*

HISTORY, CULTURE & THOUGHT
Dr. **Catherine Andreyev**, *University of Oxford*
Prof. **Mark Bassin**, *Södertörn University*
Prof. **Karsten Brüggemann**, *Tallinn University*
Dr. **Alexander Etkind**, *University of Cambridge*
Dr. **Gasan Gusejnov**, *Moscow State University*
Prof. em. **Walter Laqueur**, *Georgetown University*
Prof. **Leonid Luks**, *Catholic University of Eichstaett*
Dr. **Olga Malinova**, *Russian Academy of Sciences*
Prof. **Andrei Rogatchevski**, *University of Tromsø*
Dr. **Mark Tauger**, *West Virginia University*

ADVISORY BOARD*

Prof. **Dominique Arel**, *University of Ottawa*
Prof. **Jörg Baberowski**, *Humboldt University of Berlin*
Prof. **Margarita Balmaceda**, *Seton Hall University*
Dr. **John Barber**, *University of Cambridge*
Prof. **Timm Beichelt**, *European University Viadrina*
Dr. **Katrin Boeckh**, *University of Munich*
Prof. em. **Archie Brown**, *University of Oxford*
Dr. **Vyacheslav Bryukhovetsky**, *Kyiv-Mohyla Academy*
Prof. **Timothy Colton**, *Harvard University, Cambridge*
Prof. **Paul D'Anieri**, *University of Florida*
Dr. **Heike Dörrenbächer**, *Friedrich Naumann Foundation*
Dr. **John Dunlop**, *Hoover Institution, Stanford, California*
Dr. **Sabine Fischer**, *SWP, Berlin*
Dr. **Geir Flikke**, *NUPI, Oslo*
Prof. **David Galbreath**, *University of Aberdeen*
Prof. **Alexander Galkin**, *Russian Academy of Sciences*
Prof. **Frank Golczewski**, *University of Hamburg*
Dr. **Nikolas Gvosdev**, *Naval War College, Newport, RI*
Prof. **Mark von Hagen**, *Arizona State University*
Dr. **Guido Hausmann**, *University of Munich*
Prof. **Dale Herspring**, *Kansas State University*
Dr. **Stefani Hoffman**, *Hebrew University of Jerusalem*
Prof. **Mikhail Ilyin**, *MGIMO (U) MID RF, Moscow*
Prof. **Vladimir Kantor**, *Higher School of Economics*
Dr. **Ivan Katchanovski**, *University of Ottawa*
Prof. em. **Andrzej Korbonski**, *University of California*
Dr. **Iris Kempe**, *"Caucasus Analytical Digest"*
Prof. **Herbert Küpper**, *Institut für Ostrecht Regensburg*
Dr. **Rainer Lindner**, *CEEER, Berlin*
Prof. **Vladimir Malakhov**, *Russian Academy of Sciences*

Dr. **Luke March**, *University of Edinburgh*
Prof. **Michael McFaul**, *Stanford University, Palo Alto*
Prof. **Birgit Menzel**, *University of Mainz-Germersheim*
Prof. **Valery Mikhailenko**, *The Urals State University*
Prof. **Emil Pain**, *Higher School of Economics, Moscow*
Dr. **Oleg Podvintsev**, *Russian Academy of Sciences*
Prof. **Olga Popova**, *St. Petersburg State University*
Prof. **Alex Pravda**, *University of Oxford*
Dr. **Erik van Ree**, *University of Amsterdam*
Dr. **Joachim Rogall**, *Robert Bosch Foundation Stuttgart*
Prof. **Peter Rutland**, *Wesleyan University, Middletown*
Prof. **Marat Salikov**, *The Urals State Law Academy*
Dr. **Gwendolyn Sasse**, *University of Oxford*
Dr. **Jutta Scherrer**, *EHESS, Paris*
Prof. **Robert Service**, *University of Oxford*
Mr. **James Sherr**, *RIIA Chatham House London*
Dr. **Oxana Shevel**, *Tufts University, Medford*
Prof. **Eberhard Schneider**, *University of Siegen*
Prof. **Olexander Shnyrkov**, *Shevchenko University, Kyiv*
Prof. **Hans-Henning Schröder**, *SWP, Berlin*
Prof. **Yuri Shapoval**, *Ukrainian Academy of Sciences*
Prof. **Viktor Shnirelman**, *Russian Academy of Sciences*
Dr. **Lisa Sundstrom**, *University of British Columbia*
Dr. **Philip Walters**, *"Religion, State and Society"*, Oxford
Prof. **Zenon Wasyliw**, *Ithaca College, New York State*
Dr. **Lucan Way**, *University of Toronto*
Dr. **Markus Wehner**, *"Frankfurter Allgemeine Zeitung"*
Dr. **Andrew Wilson**, *University College London*
Prof. **Jan Zielonka**, *University of Oxford*
Prof. **Andrei Zorin**, *University of Oxford*

* While the Editorial Committee and Advisory Board support the General Editor in the choice and improvement of manuscripts for publication, responsibility for remaining errors and misinterpretations in the series' volumes lies with the books' authors.

Soviet and Post-Soviet Politics and Society (SPPS)
ISSN 1614-3515

Founded in 2004 and refereed since 2007, SPPS makes available affordable English-, German-, and Russian-language studies on the history of the countries of the former Soviet bloc from the late Tsarist period to today. It publishes between 5 and 20 volumes per year and focuses on issues in transitions to and from democracy such as economic crisis, identity formation, civil society development, and constitutional reform in CEE and the NIS. SPPS also aims to highlight so far understudied themes in East European studies such as right-wing radicalism, religious life, higher education, or human rights protection. The authors and titles of all previously published volumes are listed at the end of this book. For a full description of the series and reviews of its books, see www.ibidem-verlag.de/red/spps.

Editorial correspondence & manuscripts should be sent to: Dr. Andreas Umland, c/o DAAD, German Embassy, vul. Bohdana Khmelnitskoho 25, UA-01901 Kyiv, Ukraine. e-mail: umland@stanfordalumni.org

Business correspondence & review copy requests should be sent to: *ibidem* Press, Leuschnerstr. 40, 30457 Hannover, Germany; tel.: +49 511 2622200; fax: +49 511 2622201; spps@ibidem.eu.

Authors, reviewers, referees, and editors for (as well as all other persons sympathetic to) SPPS are invited to join its networks at www.facebook.com/group.php?gid=52638198614
www.linkedin.com/groups?about=&gid=103012
www.xing.com/net/spps-ibidem-verlag/

Recent Volumes

160   Mieste Hotopp-Riecke
Die Tataren der Krim zwischen Assimilation und Selbstbehauptung
Der Aufbau des krimtatarischen Bildungswesens nach Deportation und Heimkehr (1990-2005)
Mit einem Vorwort von Swetlana Czerwonnaja
ISBN 978-3-89821-940-2

161   Olga Bertelsen (ed.)
Revolution and War in Contemporary Ukraine
The Challenge of Change
ISBN 978-3-8382-1016-2

162   Natalya Ryabinska
Ukraine's Post-Communist Mass Media
Between Capture and Commercialization
With a foreword by Marta Dyczok
ISBN 978-3-8382-1011-7

163   Alexandra Cotofana, James M. Nyce (eds.)
Religion and Magic in Socialist and Post-Socialist Contexts
Historic and Ethnographic Case Studies of Orthodoxy, Heterodoxy, and Alternative Spirituality
With an afterword by Catherine Wanner
ISBN 978-3-8382-0989-0

164   Nozima Akhrarkhodjaeva
The Instrumentalisation of Mass Media in Electoral Authoritarian Regimes
Evidence from Russia's Presidential Election Campaigns of 2000 and 2008
ISBN 978-3-8382-1013-1

165   Yulia Krasheninnikova
Informal Healthcare in Contemporary Russia
Sociographic Essays on the Post-Soviet Infrastructure for Alternative Healing Practices
ISBN 978-3-8382-0970-8

166   Peter Kaiser
Das Schachbrett der Macht
Die Handlungsspielräume eines sowjetischen Funktionärs unter Stalin am Beispiel des Generalsekretärs des Komsomol Aleksandr Kosarev (1929-1938)
Mit einem Vorwort von Dietmar Neutatz
ISBN 978-3-8382-1052-0

132　Serghei Golunov
　　The Elephant in the Room
　　Corruption and Cheating in Russian Universities
　　ISBN 978-3-8382-0570-0

133　Manja Hussner, Rainer Arnold (Hgg.)
　　Verfassungsgerichtsbarkeit in Zentralasien I
　　Sammlung von Verfassungstexten
　　ISBN 978-3-8382-0595-3

134　Nikolay Mitrokhin
　　Die "Russische Partei"
　　Die Bewegung der russischen Nationalisten in der UdSSR 1953-1985
　　Aus dem Russischen übertragen von einem Übersetzerteam unter der Leitung von Larisa Schippel
　　ISBN 978-3-8382-0024-8

135　Manja Hussner, Rainer Arnold (Hgg.)
　　Verfassungsgerichtsbarkeit in Zentralasien II
　　Sammlung von Verfassungstexten
　　ISBN 978-3-8382-0597-7

136　Manfred Zeller
　　Das sowjetische Fieber
　　Fußballfans im poststalinistischen Vielvölkerreich
　　Mit einem Vorwort von Nikolaus Katzer
　　ISBN 978-3-8382-0757-5

137　Kristin Schreiter
　　Stellung und Entwicklungspotential zivilgesellschaftlicher Gruppen in Russland
　　Menschenrechtsorganisationen im Vergleich
　　ISBN 978-3-8382-0673-8

138　David R. Marples, Frederick V. Mills (eds.)
　　Ukraine's Euromaidan
　　Analyses of a Civil Revolution
　　ISBN 978-3-8382-0660-8

139　Bernd Kappenberg
　　Setting Signs for Europe
　　Why Diacritics Matter for European Integration
　　With a foreword by Peter Schlobinski
　　ISBN 978-3-8382-0663-9

140　René Lenz
　　Internationalisierung, Kooperation und Transfer
　　Externe bildungspolitische Akteure in der Russischen Föderation
　　Mit einem Vorwort von Frank Ettrich
　　ISBN 978-3-8382-0751-3

141　Juri Plusnin, Yana Zausaeva, Natalia Zhidkevich, Artemy Pozanenko
　　Wandering Workers
　　Mores, Behavior, Way of Life, and Political Status of Domestic Russian Labor Migrants
　　Translated by Julia Kazantseva
　　ISBN 978-3-8382-0653-0

142　Matthew Kott, David J. Smith (eds.)
　　Latvia – A Work in Progress?
　　100 Years of State- and Nation-building
　　ISBN 978-3-8382-0648-6

143　Инна Чувычкина (ред.)
　　Экспортные нефте- и газопроводы на постсоветском пространстве
　　Анализ трубопроводной политики в свете теории международных отношений
　　ISBN 978-3-8382-0822-0

144　Johann Zajaczkowski
　　Russland – eine pragmatische Großmacht?
　　Eine rollentheoretische Untersuchung russischer Außenpolitik am Beispiel der Zusammenarbeit mit den USA nach 9/11 und des Georgienkrieges von 2008
　　Mit einem Vorwort von Siegfried Schieder
　　ISBN 978-3-8382-0837-4

145　Boris Popivanov
　　Changing Images of the Left in Bulgaria
　　The Challenge of Post-Communism in the Early 21st Century
　　ISBN 978-3-8382-0667-7

146　Lenka Krátká
　　A History of the Czechoslovak Ocean Shipping Company 1948-1989
　　How a Small, Landlocked Country Ran Maritime Business During the Cold War
　　ISBN 978-3-8382-0666-0

147　Alexander Sergunin
　　Explaining Russian Foreign Policy Behavior
　　Theory and Practice
　　ISBN 978-3-8382-0752-0

148 Darya Malyutina
     Migrant Friendships in a Super-Diverse City
     Russian-Speakers and their Social Relationships in London in the 21st Century
     With a foreword by Claire Dwyer
     ISBN 978-3-8382-0652-3

149 Alexander Sergunin, Valery Konyshev
     Russia in the Arctic
     Hard or Soft Power?
     ISBN 978-3-8382-0753-7

150 John J. Maresca
     Helsinki Revisited
     A Key U.S. Negotiator's Memoirs on the Development of the CSCE into the OSCE
     With a foreword by Hafiz Pashayev
     ISBN 978-3-8382-0852-7

151 Jardar Østbø
     The New Third Rome
     Readings of a Russian Nationalist Myth
     With a foreword by Pål Kolstø
     ISBN 978-3-8382-0870-1

152 Simon Kordonsky
     Socio-Economic Foundations of the Russian Post-Soviet Regime
     The Resource-Based Economy and Estate-Based Social Structure of Contemporary Russia
     With a foreword by Svetlana Barsukova
     ISBN 978-3-8382-0775-9

153 Duncan Leitch
     Assisting Reform in Post-Communist Ukraine 2000–2012
     The Illusions of Donors and the Disillusion of Beneficiaries
     With a foreword by Kataryna Wolczuk
     ISBN 978-3-8382-0844-2

154 Abel Polese
     Limits of a Post-Soviet State
     How Informality Replaces, Renegotiates, and Reshapes Governance in Contemporary Ukraine
     With a foreword by Colin Williams
     ISBN 978-3-8382-0845-9

155 Mikhail Suslov (ed.)
     Digital Orthodoxy in the Post-Soviet World
     The Russian Orthodox Church and Web 2.0
     With a foreword by Father Cyril Hovorun
     ISBN 978-3-8382-0871-8

156 Leonid Luks
     Zwei „Sonderwege"? Russisch-deutsche Parallelen und Kontraste (1917-2014)
     Vergleichende Essays
     ISBN 978-3-8382-0823-7

157 Vladimir V. Karacharovskiy, Ovsey I. Shkaratan, Gordey A. Yastrebov
     Towards a New Russian Work Culture
     Can Western Companies and Expatriates Change Russian Society?
     With a foreword by Elena N. Danilova
     Translated by Julia Kazantseva
     ISBN 978-3-8382-0902-9

158 Edmund Griffiths
     Aleksandr Prokhanov and Post-Soviet Esotericism
     ISBN 978-3-8382-0903-6

159 Timm Beichelt, Susann Worschech (eds.)
     Transnational Ukraine?
     Networks and Ties that Influence(d) Contemporary Ukraine
     ISBN 978-3-8382-0944-9

160 Mieste Hotopp-Riecke
     Die Tataren der Krim zwischen Assimilation und Selbstbehauptung
     Der Aufbau des krimtatarischen Bildungswesens nach Deportation und Heimkehr (1990-2005)
     Mit einem Vorwort von Swetlana Czerwonnaja
     ISBN 978-3-89821-940-2

161 Olga Bertelsen (ed.)
     Revolution and War in Contemporary Ukraine
     The Challenge of Change
     ISBN 978-3-8382-1016-2

162 Natalya Ryabinska
     Ukraine's Post-Communist Mass Media
     Between Capture and Commercialization
     With a foreword by Marta Dyczok
     ISBN 978-3-8382-1011-7

163 *Alexandra Cotofana,*
James M. Nyce (eds.)
Religion and Magic in Socialist and
Post-Socialist Contexts
Historic and Ethnographic Case Studies of
Orthodoxy, Heterodoxy, and Alternative
Spirituality
With an afterword by Catherine Wanner
ISBN 978-3-8382-0989-0

164 *Nozima Akhrarkhodjaeva*
The Instrumentalisation of Mass
Media in Electoral Authoritarian
Regimes
Evidence from Russia's Presidential Election
Campaigns of 2000 and 2008
ISBN 978-3-8382-1013-1

165 *Yulia Krasheninnikova*
Informal Healthcare in Contemporary
Russia
Sociographic Essays on the Post-Soviet
Infrastructure for Alternative Healing
Practices
ISBN 978-3-8382-0970-8

166 *Peter Kaiser*
Das Schachbrett der Macht
Die Handlungsspielräume eines sowjetischen
Funktionärs unter Stalin am Beispiel des
Generalsekretärs des Komsomol
Aleksandr Kosarev (1929-1938)
Mit einem Vorwort von Dietmar Neutatz
ISBN 978-3-8382-1052-0

ibidem.eu